Philosophy of Education:

Critical Realism
as an
Appropriate Paradigm
for a
Philosophy of Education
in
Multicultural Contexts

Glenn Rogers

Simpson & Brook, Publishers
Bedford, Texas

ISBN 0-9792072-8-2
13 Digit ISBN 978-0-9792072-8-0

Simpson & Brook, Publishers
Bedford, Texas

www.simpsonandbrookpublishers.com

TABLE OF CONTENTS

LIST OF FIGURES

INTRODUCTION

The purpose of this study is the identification of a philosophical paradigm for the Philosophy of Education that is appropriate for accomplishing citizenship education in multicultural contexts. Chapter 1 provides a historical overview of the field of Philosophy of Education, designed to identify what philosophers and educators through the ages have identified as the basic goal or purpose of education—*citizenship education*, that is, the education of individuals prepared to participate and contribute in a meaningful way to their society. Chapter 2 provides an overview of the current state and needs of our educational system given its existing and growing multicultural nature, focusing especially on the kind of training teachers need if they are to accomplish citizenship education in a multicultural context. Chapter 3 provides a discussion of what Critical Realism is and demonstrates how and why it is an appropriate paradigm for accomplishing citizenship education in multicultural contexts.

CHAPTER 1

PHILOSOPHY OF EDUCATION
A HISTORICAL OVERVIEW

Since the days of Socrates, leading philosophers have believed that the purpose of education is to assist in the moral as well as the intellectual and social development of individuals who can participate in society in meaningful, productive ways. This section will provide an overview of the ideas and opinions of leading philosophers on the purposes and processes of education.

Socrates/Plato

To consider Plato's views on education is to consider Socrates' views as well, for Plato's writing provides Socrates a voice he would not otherwise have enjoyed. Since in this blending

7

of voices it is impossible to determine where the ideas of Socrates end and those of Plato begin, the ideas voiced in this section are credited to Plato, though he may well be voicing ideas that originated with Socrates.

David Cooper notes that for both Socrates and Plato, morality was the most important business of philosophy and of life. The morally good life was the only route to happiness and fulfillment (10). That the teaching of morality (that is, *the care of the soul*[1]) was, for Plato, a foundational concern of education can be seen in *Protagoras,* when Socrates challenges the Sophists' ability to teach young people to live properly given their (the Sophists') subjectivist or relativist views (D. Cooper 11). To put it bluntly, how can one teach virtue if one does not know what virtue is (J. Cooper 745-746)? For Plato, morality (care of the soul) and virtue (inner excellence) were both the subject and goal of education.

It is in the context of *Republic,* however, where Plato describes his ideal State that he constructs the educational framework in which morality and virtue can be imparted to students. Children, adolescents, and young adults, some of whom

---

[1] Their concept of morality, or the care of the soul, involved being the best person one could be, understanding oneself, developing one's full potential, thriving. This kind of life allowed one to be happy. It was the good life and therefore a moral life.

will become the philosopher-kings that will guide the state, will be educated through a state-controlled system that would supervise the entire process. Gruber provides a basic overview of Plato's educational system:

> The earliest years were to be spent in public nurseries, developing physical health and absorbing accepted ideas of religion and patriotism. More formal education would begin at six and continue to eighteen, when a series of examinations separate iron and copper, workmen from gold and silver upper classes. For boys between eighteen and twenty, the courses would be military. The soldier class could be eliminated at the end of this course. For the philosopher-rulers, education would continue until thirty, when an examination would eliminate the less brilliant, who would be assigned administrative posts in the government. The next five years would be spent by the most brilliant in a study of pure abstractions with the goal of catching a vision of the "Idea of the Good." From thirty-five to fifty, these philosopher-kings would rule the state in minor offices, and at fifty the most brilliant would be elected to the full status of Guardian. (4)[2]

In Book VI of *Republic*, Plato stresses the importance of a rationalistic foundation for life (and therefore for education), and in Book VII, in his parable of the cave, he links education to insight into the world beyond that which is accessible to the senses,

---

[2] It is important to remember that in the section of the Republic referred to by Gruber, Plato is describing what he considers appropriate education and training for potential rulers of what he considers the ideal State, a State that is not democratic, but what he would call aristocratic. We might call it authoritarian. While contemporary Western education may not be aiming at the education and training of an aristocratic ruling class, and while the difference between Plato's goals and ours may be significant, Plato's curriculum was designed to prepare individuals for the highest civil service and is, therefore, a relevant consideration in this discussion.

which for Plato is the real world of Ideas, the absolute realities upon which the material forms are based, ultimate universals such as truth, beauty, justice, and so forth. For Plato, education is the *role* process that <u>allows individuals access</u> to that which is really real and therefore of the highest value, exposing and clarifying that which is of the highest good, that which is truly virtuous and moral. A society of people thus educated would be a society that reflected that which is true and beautiful and good, in which individuals could experience fulfillment as productive members of the *polis*. For Plato, the <u>goal of education</u> is to produce a productive, moral citizen who can contribute to the productivity and morality of society. For Plato, the goal of education was to produce a good citizen.

Aristotle

Though Aristotle disagreed with his teacher, Plato, regarding the unseen universals Plato called *Ideas*, the two held similar opinions regarding the importance of a moral life rooted in rationality. In *Nicomachean Ethics*, Aristotle said, "for man… the life according to reason is the best and pleasantest, since reason more than anything else *is* man," (Bk. X: Ch. 7, 1178). While Plato's dualist perspective (the material world versus the world of Ideas) was focused on understanding the more important world of

Ideas, a realm unavailable to the senses, Aristotle, in contrast, was focused on understanding the physical world. For Aristotle, knowledge began with sense perception.[3] The things perceived by the senses, however, must be understood through inductive reasoning.

Because of their different approaches to metaphysics and epistemology, some have labeled Plato an idealist and Aristotle a realist (Hobson 15). However, when it comes to the purposes and goals of life and of education the two philosophers have similar perspectives. Hobson notes that in *Nicomachean Ethics* Aristotle asks and answers the question, "what is the purpose of humankind?" Aristotle's answer is *to seek happiness*, which for him had to do with doing well, with thriving. He considered this the *sole self-sufficient good.* How does one achieve this? For Aristotle, doing well, thriving, being happy, is achieved by living a virtuous life (16). The Greek word translated virtue or virtuous is *arête*, meaning *inner excellence* or *fitness for purpose.* How are young people to acquire this fitness for the ultimate human purpose, for thriving, for being happy? They achieve it through the acquisition of moral virtue.

---

[3] Plato would not have disagreed with this.

Aristotle believed that moral virtue was acquired through practice. One becomes a moral person by being a moral person. Education, then, guided by both parents and teachers, is a process of guidance in appropriate moral behavior, designed to produce a moral person who will thrive and contribute to the morality, and therefore the thriving, of society (17). This moral guidance for young children allows them to establish patterns of behavior that can, later on, be translated into "principled moral action" as abstract conceptual abilities develop. Psychologists of the modern era such as Piaget and Kohlberg have demonstrated that Aristotle was right in this regard (18).

Aristotle's basic framework for a complete education was similar to Plato's. Early education provided moral guidance and basic skills. When intellectually capable, the child was provided with a *liberal arts* education which consisted of the kinds of subjects taught in Aristotle's Lyceum: mathematics, logic, metaphysics, ethics, politics, aesthetics, music, poetry, rhetoric, physics, and biology (18).

Though there were some fundamental philosophical distinctions between Aristotle and Plato, both believed that life must be rooted in morality and virtue, which provide the bases for doing well, for thriving. The purpose of education, therefore, for

Aristotle as well as for Plato, was to produce a virtuous, moral citizen who could contribute to the virtue and morality of society.

St. Augustine

Ronald Reed and Tony Johnson note that that which "is frequently overlooked about Augustine is his pivotal position in educational thought. He stands at the beginning of the medieval period and set the themes that will define that era. At the same time, given his pagan studies, described throughout the *Confessions*, there is a very real Platonic (or Neoplatonic) feel to Augustine's thought," (29-30). While Augustine actually preceded the Medieval period by a considerable number of years (depending on how one defines Medieval and when one dates the beginning of that period), Reed and Johnson's point is that Augustine's impact was so substantial that he laid the foundation for much of the thought of that period—even though he lived long before it actually began.

The best way to understand Augustine's approach to education and who would be considered an educated person (not only in Augustine's time but well into the Middle Ages) is to contrast the medieval conceptions regarding an educated person with those of the modern era. One of the philosophical foundations of the modern era is Cartesian doubt.[4] The modern mind seeks a solid foundation upon which to build. For Augustine, there was no need to search for a foundation. The firmest of foundations was clearly evident—God through Christ as set forth in the Holy Scriptures and believed in by a community of faith (Reed and Johnson 30-31). Yet Augustine's faith as a Christian was rooted in a Neoplatonic understanding of the cosmos in which the human experience of the material must be understood and interpreted in light of the spiritual.[5] The need to understand both realms drove not only Augustine's theology, but his philosophy of life and education as well.

It is interesting and highly significant that Reed and Johnson find a great deal of similarity between Dewey's (liberal)

---

[4] Descartes' method of doubt: "Nothing is to be admitted as true unless (a) it is free from all prejudicial judgments, and (b) it is clearly and distinctly presented to the mind that in no circumstance can it ever be doubted." From Part II of Descartes' *Discourse on Method*, quoted by Angeles (75-76).

[5] To suggest that Augustine was influenced by Neoplatonic philosophy is not to suggest that he embraced every aspect of it. Rather, that his perspectives and thinking, including the development of his theology, were influenced by it. As a Neoplatonist, Augustine was influenced by Plotinus, who, in his writing entitled *Enneads*, affirms five basic Platonic themes: "(1) the non-materiality of the highest form of reality, (2) belief that there must be a higher level of reality than visible and sensible things, (3) preference for intellectual intuition over empirical forms of knowing, (4) belief in some form of immortality, and (5) belief that the universe is essentially good. The difference, however, [between Plato and Plotinus] is that Plotinus affirms all of these as a monist interested in asserting a real identity between that natural and the supernatural both in man and throughout all nature" (Harris 649).

14

philosophy of education and Augustine's ancient philosophy of education. Augustine "recast the role of teacher from one of mere conveyor of information to one who is most concerned with creating an environment in which children are encouraged either to have new experiences or to recall old ones," (31). Indeed, a reading of Augustine's *Concerning The Teacher* (ca. 389), feels eerily modern.

P. J. Fitzpatrick suggests that Augustine's break with traditional teaching methods of his day may have been due to his own unhappy educational experiences as a child and youth (25). From an Augustinian perspective, the "teacher believes that [his or her] words [to students] become meaningful only to the extent that they can be connected with a set of experiences. Thus, she or he busies herself or himself with speaking and acting so that the classroom becomes a place in which students have experiences and are encouraged to evaluate those experiences using the criteria provided by religion" (Reed and Johnson 31).

For Augustine, then, the educated person is one who has been enabled to make sense of his or her experiences as they are interpreted through the lens of religious faith. In other words, education ought to help people make sense out of life so they can live well. The Augustinian framework for making sense of life (one could rightly say for instruction in virtue and morality) was the Christian faith, but aside from his very specific Christian frame of reference, Augustine's goals for education are very similar to those of Plato and Aristotle—the development of a moral person in the context of a social community.

Thomas Aquinas

When Aristotle's work that had been lost for centuries was rediscovered in the late Middle Ages, it shook the Christian community to its foundations because it called into question many long and dearly held assumptions and views, requiring a reevaluation of perspectives and a restructuring of beliefs. Knight compares the challenges Aristotelian philosophy brought to medieval Christianity to the challenges Darwin's theories brought to nineteenth and twentieth-century Christianity (55). Aristotelianism and medieval Christianity needed to be harmonized. Thomas Aquinas accepted the challenge.

Christian *theosophy*, so heavily influenced by Augustinian Neoplatonism, advocated the importance of the soul (the spiritual realm?), deemphasizing (at least relatively) the importance of the material realm in a way that was reminiscent of Plato's philosophy. With the rediscovery and acceptance of Aristotelianism and its intense rationalistic focus on the material world, Aquinas needed to find a way to bring the two systems (Neoplatonic Christianity and

16

Aristotelianism) together. His approach was to suggest that "faith begins when reason has reached its limit" (Gruber 38), that is, "a person should acquire as much knowledge as possible through use of human reason and then rely on faith in that realm beyond the scope of human understanding" (Knight 55).

Though Aquinas wrote a small treatise entitled *Concerning the Teacher* (or *On the Teacher*), the bulk of his work, *Summa Theologica*, is a theological treatise. Gruber, however, suggests that, "in a sense, all of his works may be considered as dealing with the philosophy of education, for he wrote a complete philosophy of life, which certainly has implications for education" (38). While it may not be prudent to see philosophy of education everywhere in Aquinas' work, there are considerations worthy of note. Along with Aristotle, Aquinas believed that the physical world is understood through a process that begins with the physical senses. Aquinas advocated training in sense observation and experimentation. He believed intellectual and theoretical pursuits to be superior to practical concerns. He was clear that the purpose of education is to develop the whole person (intellectual and spiritual) by the drawing out all of the student's capabilities to create a harmonious whole person, the end result being *sanctity* (Gruber 38-39), which for Aquinas had to do with living properly as a Christian.

17

For Aquinas, education was a process designed to engage the whole person, to assist that person in becoming the best person he or she could become. Because Christianity is lived in a community context, the purpose of education is to produce a person who can live effectively and meaningfully in community. Through the idea of community in Aquinas' work the idea of citizenship emerges. Granted, it may be a somewhat different community than Plato and Aristotle had in mind,[6] but a community nonetheless, and thus the concept of citizenship is clearly part of Aquinas' thinking regarding the purpose of education.

Rousseau

In Nell Noddings' overview of the philosophy of education, she deals with Socrates and Plato and then skips right to Jean-Jacques Rousseau. Her explanation is that in her presentation of philosophy of education she is looking for philosophical/educational ideas that were not only intriguing when they were first presented, but which are still intriguing (or *besetting*) today (13).

---

[6] Plato's and Aristotle's community was the Greek *polis* rather than the church. But regardless of the specific context, polis or church, the purpose and function of community remains the same.

Emile is Rousseau's novel in which he presents his ideas on education. Timothy O'Hagan refers to *Emile* as "one of the greatest works on developmental psychology" (55). Reed and Johnson offer the following insightful (though lengthy) summary of Rousseau's philosophy of education. Please note the ultimate goal or end result of Rousseau's educational proposal.

> Nature is the key to Rousseau's educational process. According to Rousseau, a young child is apolitical, asocial, and amoral. Initially the child knows only that she or he inhabits a physical world and quickly learns to abide by the law of necessity. Rousseau suggests the young child should never act from obedience but only from necessity. In the early stages of her or his development, the child should be dependent only on things. As Emile develops under the skillful manipulation of his tutor (Rousseau himself), he internalizes the notion that restraints are natural and inevitable. Once this lesson is learned, and as Emile develops an appreciation for the moral, political, and social worlds he inhabits and the laws that govern these worlds, this properly educated individual comes to understand and appreciate the general will or common good. In short, what Rousseau offers us in Emile is the prototype of what human beings could and should be. Through an educational process that follows nature, Rousseau creates for us an exemplar, that is, a just human being in an unjust world. By emulating nature in the education of our children and youth, Rousseau is suggesting that it is possible to develop a society of Emiles who willingly sublimate their own desires to those of the common or general will. It is these individuals who will establish the just or good society by creating the social contract, in the process resolving once and for all the conflict between individual needs and societal demands. (65)

Rousseau's desire was to educate the whole person, but in a way that he believed was more in harmony with natural maturation processes. His desire was also to create a mature, holistically educated person who would put the general will (the common needs and good of society) above his or her own self interests. In other words, even though Rousseau is suggesting a divergent route for arriving at his educational destination, his destination (his purpose or desired result) has to do with the preparation of the individual for productive participation in society. It is obvious that Rousseau proposes a very different approach to accomplish his educational aims, but his aim for the overall process—producing a productive citizen—is not different from those who have gone before him.

Dewey

John Dewey was born the same year Charles Darwin published his *Origin of Species* (1859), and was greatly influenced by Darwin (Noddings 23). Dewey was a naturalistic philosopher who accepted the basic premise espoused by Heraclitus that the only certainty was the law of change (Gruber 183-184). Within that basic philosophical framework, Dewey believed education, as an integral part of the process of living, was a process of change, of growth, and that such growth could be described as the purpose of education. From this point of view, education "is a process of living and not preparation for future living" (Reed and Johnson 94). The process of experience, analysis, interpretation, enlightenment, and changed perspective is the process of education.

For Dewey, since education is part of the process of growth and change that characterizes life (or that *is* life), it is essential that the student participate in his or her own education. Dewey believed education to be "a continual process of reconstruction of experience." He felt that an educated person is a "sense-maker," that is, "one who can wrest as much meaning as possible from her or his experience" (Reed and Johnson 90).

From a sociopolitical perspective, Dewey was an advocate of participatory democracy, believing that the very idea of democracy requires those who advocate it work to "build communities in which the necessary opportunities and resources are available for every individual to fully realize his or her particular capacities and powers through participation in political, social, and cultural life" (89). Building such communities would, of necessity, include educating children in ways that give them age appropriate meaningful opportunities to participate in the political, social, and cultural life of the community. From Dewey's perspective, as children live in community, participating in the democratic life of that community, having input into the processes of growth and change, they are being educated in and for democracy.

In this sense, Dewey's purposes or aims of education are in line with the philosophers examined previously. Dewey's *child-centered* approach, in which children participate in their own education, is rooted in the meaningful participation in a democratic community in which the individual has the opportunity to "fully realize his or her particular capacities and powers through participation" in the community. Is this not another way of suggesting the purpose of education is the growth and development of the individual for meaningful participation in society? Dewey proposed different ways of conceiving and accomplishing the process of education, but his goals were essentially the same as educational philosophers who had gone before him, educating children in such a way and so that they might be productive citizens.

Noddings

For twenty-three years Nel Noddings was a primary and secondary school teacher, earning her Ph.D. in Educational Philosophy and Theory in 1973 from Stanford University when she was forty-four. Because of her own educational experiences of having a few key teachers who cared deeply for her, and because of her experience as a teacher who cared deeply about her students, Noddings proposes that education must be carried out in a caring

22

environment where the moral development of children is foundational. This is accomplished in a context of caring that includes four processes: 1) *modeling*, that is, showing children what it means to care, 2) *dialog*, talking about caring, 3) *practice* in caring for others and reflection on that caring, and 4) *confirmation* or affirmation, that is, encouraging the best in others (Noddings 226-230).

For Noddings, education must be individualistically child-centered. It must be centered in the needs, interests, and abilities of each child. Not all children can learn every subject equally well, neither are they equally interested in all subjects (251). Teachers, then, must be *care-givers*, caring enough about students to identity and understand their needs, interests, strengths, and weaknesses and to help children not only learn what they need to learn (which for Noddings includes traditional educational subject matter), but to become caring people. When teachers, through modeling, dialog, practice, and confirmation teach children to be caring people, society can be transformed into a more caring society (255). Her educational goal is the moral development of the child in a loving environment, which will enable the child to achieve his or her potential as a caring person in a caring society. In this regard, the purpose of education is the moral development of the individual for the mutual benefit of the individual and of society. It is essentially the same goal of the philosophers who preceded her—moral and meaningful citizenship.

Summary

Over the centuries, theories about how to educate children have been developed, defended, discarded, and resurrected or reincarnated. Plato and Aristotle have had lasting influence from the perspective of subject matter, while Rousseau has probably had more influence than many realize regarding methodology, with his novel *Emile* providing the foundation for progressive child-centered approaches. Yet for all the differences in methodology, there is a unity of purpose that pervades educational theory from ancient times to the present. It is the idea (in the broadest terms) that the purpose of education is to prepare an individual for moral and meaningful participation in society, or as James Banks prefers, *citizenship education.*

For the ancients, a moral person was one focused on inner excellence. A moral person was a happy, thriving person, fulfilling his purpose in life. This was considered a virtuous life. Education ought to prepare a person for a moral life, one of meaningful participation in society, reaching one's full potential as a person, and thereby participating and contributing constructively to the social community of which one is a part. How, exactly, this purpose is to be achieved will require protracted and detailed discussions. A complicating contemporary issue that must be considered in the discussion is how citizenship education occurs in a multicultural, pluralistic social context.

CHAPTER 2

CITIZENSHIP EDUCATION

Citizenship education is about preparing individuals for meaningful participation in society. It is an education that encompasses the entire range of skills and perspectives necessary to negotiate the complexities of a contemporary social context, which in the West is not only highly technological but increasingly multicultural and pluralistic in nature. My goals in this chapter are: 1) to identify the nature of citizenship education in a multicultural context, 2) to identify the perspectives, insights and skills educators must possess to accomplish citizenship education in a multicultural context, and 3) to suggest the specific kind of preparation educators need in order to be adequately prepared to work effectively in multicultural contexts. To accomplish these goals it will be helpful to begin with some brief introductory comments about America's contemporary social context and the response of the educational community to those realities before looking specifically at issues related to effective multicultural education.

The Multicultural Realities of America's Educational Context

The United States is an Anglo-dominant culture with approximately 70% of the population being Anglo.[7] The remaining 30% of the population is comprised of non-Anglo peoples. Latinos comprise the largest minority population (approaching 15%) with African Americans being a slightly smaller group. The gap between Latinos and African Americans,

---

[7] *Anglo* is a broad ethnic designation referring to white people of Western European cultural heritage. Generally speaking it refers to white people but focuses not on the phenotypical characteristics such as skin color, the shape of facial features, or the texture of one's hair, but on broad cultural similarities, which includes worldviews. As an ethnic group, Anglos are distinct from Latinos, Africans, African Americans, Asians, Indians, Native Americans, and so forth. Anglo as an ethnic designation is sometimes used simply as a replacement term for the racial designation of White. In this sense it is no more accurate than the racial designation, for not all "White" people are of Western European cultural heritage. However, from an anthropological perspective, a broad ethnic designation such as Anglo, though not as precise as one might prefer, is preferable to a racial designation, which is virtually meaningless because it is an identification of nothing more than phenotypical traits. Culture makes people who and what they are, not their phenotypical traits. Ethnic designations, therefore, are preferable to phenotyically rooted racial designations.

however, will continue to widen and Latinos will be by far the largest minority group in the U.S. It is estimated that by 2050 only 50% of the U.S. population will be Anglo (Rogers 2006, 15-27).

The cultural diversity that characterizes our society, especially as a result of immigration, along with the substantial African American presence and the diversification dynamic associated with it, impacts significantly the process of education in our society. As the 30% non-Anglo population moves steadily toward 50% and beyond, issues related to multicultural education will only become more significant. There are many questions that need to be considered. The issue at hand is, how does the multicultural nature of contemporary American society impact a philosophy of education?

Education in Multicultural Perspective

James Banks notes that "[m]ulticultural education is a reform movement designed to make some major changes in the education of students" (2008, 1). The concept of multicultural education

> came into being initially as a pragmatic response, based on broadly liberal principles, to a number of practical educational issues that surfaced in the last 30 to 40 years as a result of the increasing cultural and ethnic diversity within Western states. Subsequent philosophical attention to the concept has begun to explore its social and political ramifications more fully and to link it to more recent cultural theory,

and as a result a more substantial body of theory is beginning to develop around the concept. (Dhillon and Halstead 146)

To understand the philosophy of multicultural education one must consider the goals that appear to represent mainstream thinking within the field. Banks, probably the leading scholar in the discipline of multicultural education, refers often to "citizenship education" as a goal of education in general and of multicultural education as well (1997, 1-2). His understanding of citizenship education is deeply rooted in democracy and the need for citizens to be able to participate in democratic society in meaningful ways. But since "people are not born democrats... an important goal of the schools in a democratic society is to help students acquire the knowledge, values, and skills needed to participate effectively in public communities" (1). In this regard, Banks places himself in the company of numerous Western philosophers, echoing their views on the purpose and goals of education. In referring to "education for democratic citizenship," Kenneth Cushner, Averil McClelland, and Philip Stafford align themselves in this same tradition (130).

The Goals of Multicultural Education

Beyond this very broad conceptualization of citizenship education, what are the specific goals of multicultural education? Banks discuses seven goals of multicultural education (2008:2-5):

1. To assist students in gaining deeper self-understanding by seeing themselves from the perspectives of other cultures, assuming also that greater insight into other cultures will generate respect for other cultures.

2. To provide students with cultural, ethnic, and language alternatives, avoiding the harmful consequences (for ethnically-other students) of a curriculum that is Anglocentric.

3. To provide all students with the skills, attitudes, and knowledge needed to function within their own culture, within the mainstream culture, and across culture boundaries.

4. To reduce the pain and discrimination that ethnically-other people experience because of their unique characteristics. The "pain" Banks refers to grows out of the alienation from one's ethnic group and even oneself that is often required of the ethnically-other to succeed in an Anglo-dominant society.

5. To help students acquire the basic skills (reading, writing, math) needed to function effectively in a global and "flat" technological world—that is, one in which students from Western contexts must compete for jobs against students from developing world countries.

6. To help students understand their own cultural context but also free them from the limitations of a single cultural perspective, assisting them in the development of the knowledge, attitudes, and skills necessary for participation in civic action aimed at a more equitable and just society.

7. To help students acquire the knowledge, attitudes, and skills necessary for participation not only in local, regional, and national cultures but in global cultures and communities as well.

This is a challenging agenda, to say the least. Evidently, teachers in some contexts have their hands full just teaching the basics of reading, writing, and arithmetic. Is it realistic to expect them to also prepare students for responsible multicultural social participation? Responsible, meaningful social participation has been a foundational goal of education since the days of Socrates if not before. Does the addition of a multicultural context make the expectation unrealistic? Proponents of multicultural education would say, no. In fact, they stress that it is critical. Cushner, McClelland, and Safford link America's multicultural educational context with global educational perspectives in such a way as to suggest that the two are not separate issues, but different perspectives of the same issue. They note that:

> Education for a global perspective helps individuals better comprehend their own condition in the community and world and make more accurate and effective judgments about other people and about

31

common issues. It emphasizes the study of nations, cultures, and civilizations, including our own pluralistic society, and focuses on understanding how these are interconnected, how they change, and what individuals' roles and responsibilities are in such a world. An education with a global perspective provides a realistic, balanced perspective on world issues, as well as an awareness of how enlightened self-interest includes concerns about people elsewhere in the world. The catchphrase, "Think globally, act locally" has served the field of social studies education well. Making global concerns concrete, immediate, and meaningful to students is difficult yet critical. (254)

Banks' goals for multicultural education and the global education discussed by Cushner, McClellend, and Safford are similar. How can such goals be met? What methodological approaches to preparation for teachers and curriculum for students would be necessary for meaningful multicultural or global education to occur?

The Methodological Demands of Multicultural Education

Training teachers how to teach in a multicultural context and identifying the models that will be most effective for accomplishing the goals of citizenship education are fundamental concerns of multicultural education. A brief overview of multicultural teaching models will pave the way for a discussion of training teachers to teach in multicultural contexts.

Curriculum and Teaching Models

article about teacher training and effective teaching models (for multicultural education), Charles Jenks, James Lee, and Barry Kanpol discuss four models of multicultural curriculum and pedagogy suggested by Banks. The approaches they highlight are: *contributions, additive, transformative, and social action.* They note that the four models sometimes "blur distinctions," sometimes "overlap," and occasionally reflect only a single perspective. Taken together, however, they suggest that the four models "offer a variety of approaches… to moving schools toward a multiculturalism that is transformative in its inclusion of the voices and experiences of all students" (24). If enacted, the changes represent a transformation of methodology and content that is essential for successful citizenship education in a multicultural social context.

A brief overview of the four approaches to multicultural education (outlined by Banks, discussed by Jinks, Lee, and Kanpol) will provide a basic framework for some observations concerning an effective philosophy of education in multicultural contexts.

The first approach to multicultural education in Banks' list is the *contributions* approach. The contributions approach includes material in the standard curriculum that emphasizes the contributions minority groups (that is, individuals representative of a minority group) have made to society. Studying the social, political, economic, literary, educational, or cultural contributions African Americans, Chinese, Native Americans, and Latinos have made to American society allows students to see the value and positive impact non-Anglo people have had on American culture. The method avoids an Anglocentric approach to education by highlighting the significant contributions of non-Anglos to various areas of American society.

Second is the *additive* approach. Additive is descriptive of this approach because aspects of multicultural education that had previously been missing or ignored are added to the curriculum to provide the balance that is missing. If, for instance, it is discovered that the contributions of African Americans serving in elected offices are not being appropriately stressed those contributions can be added to the curriculum of government of social studies classes.

Third is the *transformative* approach. The transformative approach, rather than merely tacking on references to the social contributions of non-Anglo people, seeks to change the internal structure of curriculum to incorporate into the curriculum the racial, ethnic, and social experience of different minority groups. For example, when studying the family (perhaps as a segment of a social studies course), the structures, perspectives, and experiences of different kinds of families (African American, Latino, Chinese and so forth) would be included so students have an opportunity to think about family structures and norms from different ethnic and cultural perspectives.

Fourth is the *social action* approach. This approach is an extension of the transformative approach in that students are asked not only to think more broadly and to understand but also to act, to seek social justice and equity in meaningful ways. This is the most challenging of the four approaches because a school cannot realistically adopt a curriculum that challenges students to act without providing those students with opportunities and avenues for the kind of social action being encouraged.

These four approaches to multicultural education curriculum represent different levels of commitment to multicultural education. The *additive* and *contribution* approaches provide minimal exposure to multicultural realities and will result in minimal responses and changes to the status quo. The *transformative* and *social action* approaches, as described by Banks, will inform and challenge students more thoroughly but are more difficult to implement.

These approaches are rooted in a philosophy of education that is dedicated to educating students for meaningful participation in a multicultural American democratic society. The key to making citizenship education meaningful in a multicultural context involves embracing the ethnic diversity that already characterizes schools in America and including the perspectives and experiences of ethnically-other peoples (and therefore of the students themselves) in a curriculum specifically designed for that purpose. As noted, the *transformative* and *social action* approaches accomplish this purpose more effectively.

However, as important as curriculum is as a methodological concern in multicultural education, an even more fundamental concern is teacher training. Multicultural curricula alone, even when taught by teachers trained in its use, will not provide the atmosphere of acceptance and appreciation of social diversity necessary to accomplish effective multicultural citizenship education without the teachers themselves being thoroughly educated and experienced in the anthropological realities of our multicultural society.

Jenks, Lee, and Kanpol recognize the role of teacher training in multicultural education and address the issue (25). However, their suggestion for the "cross-cultural competency" of teachers appears to involve little more than teacher training related to the philosophical strengths and weaknesses of the various approaches to multicultural education. They address the need for *introspection* and *reconceptualization* of multicultural education, but their comments are rooted in reconceptualization and introspection regarding the educational process not in new insights for teachers regarding the worldviews and cultures represented in the classroom. It will take considerably more than a couple of courses in multicultural teaching methods to prepare teachers to accomplish multicultural citizenship education in contemporary American society. It will take considerable anthropological education (more than an *Introduction To* course) to prepare teachers for effective multicultural citizenship education in our contemporary social context. While some might question whether or not considerable anthropological training for teachers is realistic, perhaps we ought to be asking if it is realistic to put teachers in an ethnically diverse context without considerable anthropological training? Other than a thorough mastering of the subject matter they teach, what is more crucial for teachers to understand the cultural-specific psychosocial needs of the students they teach? If teacher training needs to be reconceived and restructured to include considerable anthropological training, then is it realistic not to do so?

Reconceptualizing the educational process and having appropriate multicultural curricula are essential for effective citizenship education. But even more fundamental is the

37

anthropologically informed cross-cultural perspective of the teacher interacting with an ethnically diverse student population. Teachers with a monocultural perspective, that is, those who lack personal experience and insight into other cultures, cannot be fully effective in multicultural education. Teachers cannot teach that which is beyond their personal frame of reference.

Training Teachers for Effective Multicultural Interactions

One of the most daunting tasks of multicultural citizenship education is preparing teachers, most of whom are middle class Anglos (Cushner, McClelland, and Safford 11), for the challenges they will face in multicultural classrooms. Valerie Duarte and Thomas Reed note that "teachers cannot be expected to be culturally responsive in the classroom, however, if they are not adequately prepared with the necessary knowledge, skills, and dispositions" (26). They go on to note that "most universities require teacher candidates to take at least one course on multiculturalism... sometimes at the beginning of the teacher education program. However, these courses may offer no more than a general awareness of the differences among cultures" (26). Attempts are being made to prepare teachers for the intercultural experiences they will have in their classrooms, but the steps taken so far, because of a lack of anthropological training, are woefully inadequate.

James Jupp, in an article entitled *Culturally Relevant Teaching*, (52-61) approaches the challenge of preparing teachers for intercultural interaction from an anthropological perspective, stressing the use of *autoethnographic reflexivity*, that is, an interactive dialog between teachers and students designed to create and inform an interactive relationship. His insights are excellent as far as they go. His *culturally relevant teaching* offers teachers a framework for understanding and addressing multicultural issues but falls short of providing teachers with the deeper kinds of insights and experience necessary for the kind of intercultural interaction and teaching necessary for thorough, effective multicultural citizenship education.

In order for teachers to be thoroughly prepared for intercultural interaction and the rigors of multicultural citizenship education, they need to complete coursework (perhaps in the context of an in-service training program) in cultural anthropology in general, and specific cultural studies of the primary cultural groups that are present in their classrooms—Latino cultures or Asian cultures, for example, depending on the student population of a given school. They need to be familiar not only with the surface-level cultural patterns of those cultures, but also with the underlying worldview assumptions that give shape to those cultures. For this to be maximally effective, teachers need to understand the cultural-specific needs of students in their local community and school context. Thus, some of their anthropological training needs to be accomplished in the local context of a specific ethnic community.

To clarify and illustrate what I mean, that is, to demonstrate how complex multicultural matters are and show why teachers need specific anthropological training, the following sections will provide an anthropological perspective on the role of worldview as it relates to culture. The realities described in the following sections are highly significant factors in every multicultural classroom.

Understanding Culture[8]

In 1871 E. B. Tylor defined culture as that *"complex whole which includes knowledge, belief, art, morals, law, customs, and any other capabilities and habits acquired by man as a member of society"* (Carrithers 1997:98). Anthropologists today still refer to this early definition of culture. Paul Hiebert's definition is a little

---

[8] The material in the following sections was originally prepared by the author for publication in, *Understanding American Culture: The Theological and Philosophical Shaping of the American Worldview,* Mission and Ministry Resources, 2006.

less cumbersome: *"the integrated system of learned patterns of behavior, ideas, and products characteristic of a society"* (1983:25).

Culture is a complex whole, an integrated system. It involves beliefs, ideas, knowledge, behaviors, morals (values), laws, customs, habits and more. Culture is basically everything about a group of people. Culture is the way a people live their lives. It involves the actual things they do and the way they do them, how they: eat, sleep, dress, get married, work, play, have babies, raise children, bury their dead, dance, worship, buy, sell, trade, think, teach, learn, mourn, laugh, fight, relax and more. Everything people do and how they do it is part of their culture. So are the underlying assumptions about life that result in what a people do and how they do it.

Analyzing Culture

That culture involves the assumptions and beliefs that lead to behaviors as well as the behaviors themselves means that there is more than one level to culture. In fact, there are at least three levels to every society's culture. Culture is a three-tiered phenomenon made up: 1) of our *deep-level* assumptions about the world and about how life is to be lived (called *worldview*), 2) of our *mid-level* internal responses, including our values and ways of

41

feeling and thinking that grow out of our deep-level worldview assumptions, and 3) of our *surface-level* behaviors and structures. Figure 1 illustrates this three-tiered view of culture.

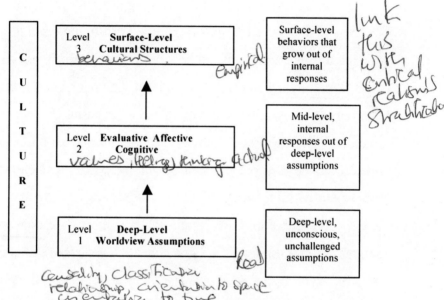

FIGURE 1: THREE-TIERED VIEW OF CULTURE

Level-three, surface-level cultural structures and behaviors, is that part of culture that we see and experience with our senses. Surface-level culture is external. It is what we eat, how we dress, drive a car, go to the bank, grocery shop, go to a movie, vote—all the things we do as we live life. These are our cultural *behaviors*. Cultural *structures* are the institutions we create that provide a framework for daily living: schools for educating our children, hospitals for caring for the sick. Our economic system is a cultural institution, so is marriage. Democracy is a cultural institution.

Surface-level institutions and behaviors are related. If democracy is a cultural institution, voting is a cultural behavior. If our educational system is a cultural institution, sending our children to school is a cultural behavior. If capitalism is a cultural institution, buying a car is a cultural behavior. Our cultural behaviors are usually accomplished in relation to a cultural structure. The cultural structures provide a context or framework for cultural behaviors. Structures and behaviors are the visible parts of our culture.

Level-two, mid-level internal responses, are the values, feelings, and thinking that lay just beneath the surface of behaviors and structures. In the West, we teach our children that cheating on a test is wrong. That is a cultural behavior we engage in. Why do we do that? Because we believe cheating is wrong. Our behaviors grow out of our values, our feelings, our thinking. When we have a headache we take medicine designed to produce a specific chemical reaction in our bodies to reduce or eliminate the pain in our heads. Why would we do that? In some other cultures a person might go to a witch doctor to have a curse removed that he or she believes is causing the headache. Why would our surface-level cultural behavior be different from that of other cultural groups? Because our mid-level internal responses are different from those of other cultural groups. We have different values. We think differently and we feel differently about things. The way we think and feel about things determines how we behave.

Our mid-level internal responses drive our surface-level behaviors and the structures we have created in relation to them. Level-two determines level-three. But where do these level-two values, feelings, and thinking come from? I have called them mid-level internal *responses*—responses to what? Our mid-level internal values, feelings, and thinking develop in response to our deep-level (level-one) unconscious assumptions about reality, about how life ought to be lived. These deep-level assumptions are referred to as *worldview*.

Worldview: What it Is, What it Does

The word *worldview* is used rather freely to refer to all sorts of things. This is unfortunate because when a word means too many things it does not really mean anything very specific. Usually when people use the word worldview they mean perspective. Often they are thinking of a particular philosophical or theological perspective or point of view. Their communication would be more accurate if they would simply use the word perspective.

Worldview, as it us used anthropologically, is a very precise term that refers to *the deep-level unconscious assumptions a people have about reality, about the nature of the world and about how life is to be lived* (Kraft 1996:52). Worldview, whether on the individual level or the societal level, allows people to understand themselves in relation to the world, and provides them with a framework for interpreting and living life.

Worldview: A Closer Look

Worldview is *the unconscious, deep-level assumptions people have about reality as they perceive it, assumptions about how the world works and how to relate to and interact with all the things, events and people encountered in life* (Rogers 2002:27).

Worldview is, for most people, an unconscious feature of who they are. Most people are not even aware of their deep-level assumptions about reality. Hiebert has noted that worldview is "what we think with, not what we think about" (1996:142). I will elaborate on the "*what we think with*" part of his comment later. For now the point is that people are unaware of their underlying assumptions about reality.

As children we learn our worldview as we grow. We learn it in our specific social and cultural context. Actually, the word *absorb* may be a better word to describe the process. We do not

45

learn our worldview the way we learn the multiplication tables. No one sits us down to teach us worldview. For the most part, worldview is *transmitted* to us informally and unintentionally within our cultural context as we listen to and observe our parents or other significant people in our lives. As we listen, observe, and experience we learn and form impressions about living life in our cultural context. On those occasions when our parents specifically instruct us, *this is what we believe and this is what we do*, we are being intentionally taught and portions of our worldview are being formed. However, worldview is not normally transmitted from one generation to another in intentional teaching situations.

The impressions we form as we grow become assumptions about life. We do not question these assumptions. We simply accept them. For instance, if we grow up in a family that prays to God, we accept the idea of God, usually, without questioning it. We hear our parents talking to God and we hear the kinds of things they thank him for and ask him to do and we form impressions that become assumptions about an invisible, all-powerful being who is actively involved in his world and who cares about and intervenes in the lives of people. As children we cannot articulate our assumptions in theological terms, but the assumptions are there. It does not occur to us to question our assumptions about God because that is the nature of assumptions—we simply assume them to be true.

We do not often think about our deep-level assumptions about reality so they remain *unconscious*. For instance, if you ask the average American about his assumptions regarding time, he will not be able to tell you. This is not because he doesn't think about time. Americans think about time all the time! But most of us do not think about our *assumptions* regarding time. We don't think about how we perceive time, why we think of it the way we do, which happens to be different from the way many other people in the world think about time. Most people don't spend a lot of time thinking about their deep-level worldview assumptions.

These deep-level worldview assumptions are about our *perceptions of reality*, assumptions about how the world works and about how life is to be lived. Our assumptions about the nature of reality have to do with a number of important and very basic considerations. What is the world like? How does it work? And, most importantly, what is my place in it? Because humans, by nature, are very focused on themselves, questions about how the world works are rooted in the basic *Self-Other* dichotomy. There is me (*Self*) and there is everything and everyone else (*Other*). What is my relationship to or with every thing and every one else?

What is the relationship of the *Self* to the *Other*? Figure 2 illustrates this *Self-Other* dichotomy.

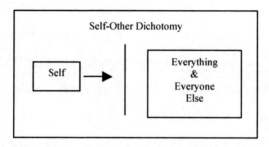

FIGURE 2: SELF-OTHER DICHOTOMY

Within the framework of this basic *Self-Other* dichotomy, lots of questions are asked and answered. The answers exist in the form of assumptions we develop as our worldview is being formed. The questions are not always framed in the context of the *Self*, but the *Self* is always present in the background. For instance, instead of asking, w*hy do things happen to me?* we may simply ask, w*hy do things happen?* Our presence in the scenario is understood even if not specified, and the more generalized inquiry has broad implications.

The question, *why do things happen?* is one of causality. It is an inquiry into the nature of the world. Why do things happen? Do things happen because a personal being (God or gods and spirits) make them happen? Or do things happen because impersonal forces (laws of physics) generate cause and effect actions and reactions? When it rains too much and there is a flood and people die, did someone cause that to happen or did it just happen? Did God cause the flood, or is global warming to blame?

As children, we do not puzzle through these difficult questions in any kind of sophisticated formal manner. We simply form impressions and develop assumptions based on the way our parents and others around us react to the challenges of life.

Another example of how we work out the *Self-Other* dichotomy as we form our worldview assumptions about life is in the area of relationships. By the way we are treated and how we feel as a result of that treatment, we begin to form impressions regarding relationships. Who are the people that are important to me? To whom do I appear to be important? Mother probably comes first, then perhaps father, or another secondary caregiver. Eventually siblings may enter the picture and we find security (assuming everything is working as it should) in the close relationships of family. That family may be the nuclear family, parents and children, or the extended family, grandparents, aunts, uncles, cousins—everybody that can be classified as "my people." Our assumptions about relationships are part of our worldview.

These are just two examples of the kinds of basic assumptions that are involved in worldview. The sections that follow will include more detail about how worldview works and how a people's worldview assumptions (people in the collective sense) provide the foundation for their culture. For now it is important to focus on the idea that worldview is the deep-level, unconscious assumptions a person has (or a group of people have) about reality, about how the world works and their place in it. These assumptions impact us in profound ways as we live life. Our deep-level assumptions (level-one) grow into the mid-level internal values, feelings and thinking (level-two) that drive the surface-level (level-three) behaviors and structures that characterize our culture.

Worldview Universals.

Worldview assumptions can be divided into five basic categories called *universals*. They are called universals because all groups of people have assumptions about these basic life considerations. These universal categories include: causality, classification, relationship, orientation to space, and orientation to time.

Causality: Assumptions about why things happen, forces or powers in the cosmos that are somehow involved in the unfolding of day-to-day life fit into the causality universal. Are the forces or powers that cause events impersonal forces (such as gravity) and therefore beyond the influence of humans? Or are they personal beings whose choices can be influenced by human beings? If the "forces" are impersonal forces beyond the influence of humans, how do we cope with the events they cause? If the "powers" are personal beings that humans can influence, how do we go about influencing them in order to achieve the desired result? These are the kinds of questions/assumptions involved in the worldview universal category of causality.

Classification: Assumptions about how things are related, how all things in life are categorized in relation to everything else fit into the classification universal. Why would some people put an orange, a chicken's foot, and a monkey into the same category? Because for some people all three of those things are food. The way we classify people and things depends on our worldview assumptions and the values and habits that grow out of them. I would not classify my wife or children as part of the property I own. Many men from traditional societies would. In my way of classifying events that occur I have a category for "accidents" and another for "random occurrences." Many people in the world do not have an "accidents" or "random occurrences" category among their worldview assumptions. For them there are no such things as accidents or random occurrences. For those people, things happen because someone (perhaps God or a spirit or an ancestor) made them happen. Assumptions about how things are related to one another and how things are associated with and grouped together are related to the worldview universal category of classification.

Relationship: Assumptions about ourselves and the <u>kinds</u> of <u>relationships we sustain with those around</u> us fit into the relationship universal. Am I first and foremost an individual whose primary identity and value grows out of the simple fact that I exist? Or am I first and foremost part of a group of people with my identity and value growing out of my relationship with and to that group? And <u>do I view others primarily as individuals or as members of a group</u>—either my group or not my group? If my assumptions about how life is to be lived are rooted in a group orientation, who is part of my group and who is not part of my group? Who is <u>community</u> and who is not? If my worldview assumptions are rooted in an individual orientation, what level of autonomy is required? How can I be an individual and still be part of a family group? Who comes first, the <u>group or me</u>? How does a group that is made up of "individuals" function differently than a group of people who are primarily members of a group? How are decisions made? How are freedom and responsibility factored in? The kinds of issues related to the basic question, *how do I relate to other people?* fall into the relationship universal of worldview assumptions.

Orientation to space: Assumptions related to how I think about the space I occupy, my relationship to the physical space I occupy as well as to nature in general fit into the orientation to space universal. Am I part of the space I occupy or separate from it? Do I own it, use it, manage it? Or am I a part of it, like a drop of water in the ocean? Is there a space in the world that is mine or do I share the space I occupy with other people? Do I share it with all other people or only with those who are my people? How should space (mine or ours) be organized? Should it be specialized and compartmentalized or used holistically? Should buildings be round or angular? Should there be private property or should there be a community sharing of all resources? Does my orientation start with myself and go outward to other people and things, or does it begin outwardly with other people and things and move inward toward me?

For instance, consider a person with an orientation that starts with himself and goes outward. If he is walking from north to south and passes a tree, he will think in terms of the tree as being, let's say, on his right. His orientation is himself. The tree is on *his* right. He perceives his world by his presence in it. On his return walk, now going south, he will think in terms of the tree being on *his* left. The tree is in the same place. He is the one who is in a different place in relation to the tree. But since his orientation is himself, the tree is perceived to be in a different place... in relation to him. He knows the tree has not moved, but that is irrelevant. He perceives the world in relation to himself and his presence in it. This person has a *self-central focus*. He is the central focus. The world exists in relation to him. A person with a *world-central focus* making the same trips past the tree would think of the tree as the central feature, an enduring part of the bigger picture that is the point of reference rather than himself (Kearney 1984:161-164). A *self-central focus* and a *world-central focus* represent two very different orientations to the space we occupy, the world we live in. These are the kinds of questions related to the worldview universal of orientation to space.

Orientation to time: Assumptions regarding how time works and how we think about it and use time fit into the orientation to time universal. Is time like a river that flows out of the past, into the present and on into the future? Or is time like a circle of recurring events from season to season and generation to generation? If time can be compared to a tree, am I focused on the roots that reach into the past, on the trunk that is a substantial representation of the very solid present, or on the branches that reach up toward a future that is yet to unfold? Do I live my life with a past, present, or future orientation? Is life to be thought of as an ongoing series of events and relationships that occur as they unfold, moments that vary in duration and quality? Or is life to be viewed as moments to be calculated, organized, measured, and managed? Western people will answer these questions differently than non-Western people.

Which is the more important concern for most Americans, what has happened in the past, or what may happen in the future? The present is real. The future is not yet real. How much of the present should I devote to an attempt to impact a future that is not yet real and that may not become real? Am I more concerned with the quality of an event and the relationships that are created or nourished by the event? Or am I more concerned with the timeframe in which the events occur? Is it more important to be focused on where you are or where you are going to be? In the living of life and the passing of days are there relationships to be enjoyed or schedules to be kept? Is the passage of time equated with the quality of life or with productivity and profit?

Our Western orientation to time is not usually an all or nothing approach with punctuality, for example, winning out over relationships. For instance, most Americans will tell you that relationships are more important than punctuality. However, when you observe how they behave it is apparent that punctuality is often given priority over relationships. For example, a wife calls her husband at work to discuss a matter with him. He explains that he has a meeting in ten minutes and needs to pull together his notes and files. Can they discuss the matter later? Which was more important, talking to his wife or getting to the meeting fully prepared on time? The way Americans behave illustrates their true beliefs about time and how it is to be managed.

Each of these five worldview universal categories involves a number of significant and complex questions and issues that have serious implications for how we live life. Figure 3 is a diagram of worldview universals.

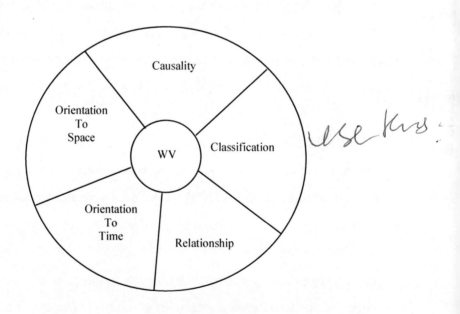

FIGURE 3: WORLDVIEW UNIVERSALS

Worldview as a Reality Filter

Our worldview serves as a reality filter. Everything we encounter in life, all the reality that we experience, gets filtered through our worldview. There is nothing that we encounter or experience (physically, emotively, cognitively) that is not experienced, judge, categorized, and responded to on the basis of our worldview assumptions. If an experience makes us happy, sad, or angry, trace the emotion back far enough (or deep enough) and you will find an assumption in one of the worldview universals that drives that emotion. Our actions and reactions, our values, our thinking and our feelings all grow out of our worldview assumptions. As we live life, our worldview assumptions (without our awareness of the process) are guiding us in how we react to that which we encounter or experience.

When we determine a thing is or is not worth our time or attention, several layers down, deep below our conscious level of awareness, our worldview is at work. Our worldview informs our value system, which in turn, tells us whether or not a thing is worth our time or attention. All of the hundreds of questions and possible responses related to worldview universals get answered based on our worldview assumptions. Our assumptions regarding the relative importance of social *harmony* versus *justice*, for example, will guide and inform our decision to seek reconciliation or discover blame and accountability. Our assumptions regarding causality (impersonal forces such as physics versus a personal being such as God, or some combination of the two) informs our thinking and feelings when we hear that hundreds or thousands of people have died in an earthquake or as a result of a volcanic eruption.

Life is lived on the basis of how experiences are filtered though our worldview. People everywhere in the world experience the same basic REALITY. But REALITY is individually and culturally perceived. The word REALITY (written in all capital letters) represents the cosmic REALITY, all there is that really happens, while the word *reality* (written in small case letters and *italicized*) represents the individual and cultural perception of REALITY.[9]

All people live in the same world, have the same physical needs and experience the same general life experiences: birth, hunger, heat, cold, fear, joy, sickness, aloneness, love, betrayal, anger, thirst, exhaustion, age, death. The same REALITY comes to us all. But what comes to us as REALITY is filtered through our culturally determined worldview and comes out as *reality*—our *reality*, a *reality* shaped, understood and dealt with on the basis of

---

[9] I am indebted to Charles Kraft for this REALITY/reality way of explaining perception (1996: 17-20).

our worldview. REALITY becomes *reality* as it passes through our worldview. This happens on an individual level. But if enough people in a given society share very similar worldview assumptions, the process then occurs on a societal or cultural level as well.

Figure 4 illustrates how different worldviews (on the societal level not the individual level), acting as *experience filters*, impact how a society experiences and interprets REALITY. Differing interpretations of REALITY result in different cultural expressions of *reality*.

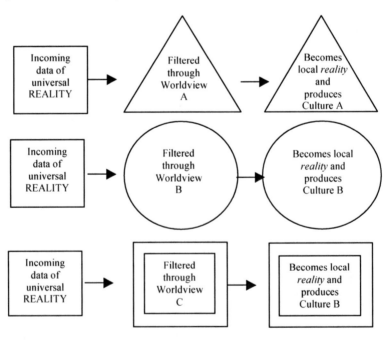

FIGURE 4: WORLDVIEW AS A REALITY FILTER

Worldview as an Interpretive Framework for Life

Not only does our worldview filter REALITY for us, in doing so it provides us with a framework for effective living, that is, for making sense out of life's experiences (Kraft 2002:7.1-17). How does one cope with the death of a loved one, with the tragedy of a deadly tornado, with the loss of a job, with social injustice, with shattered dreams, with betrayal, defeat, frustration, with the price of gasoline and of milk? How does one cope with victory, with the realization of dreams, with being in the right place at the right time, with a good income and a healthy family, with a good education and leisure time, with a good retirement fund, a nice house, nice cars, nice clothes, good food and good friends? How does one cope with the good one enjoys while so many others suffer? How does one cope with so much suffering when so many others do not have to?

Worldview assumptions help us make sense of these kinds of challenging questions—even if the answer we come up with is simply, *"It's the luck of the draw."* Worldview is at work in that answer. Whether or not the assumptions that would lead one to that conclusion are valid is another matter altogether, but worldview assumptions provide the basis for such conclusions. Our level-one worldview assumptions are the basis for our level-two internal responses (values, feelings, thinking), which are the basis for our level-three cultural structures and behaviors. The kind of funerals we have, for instance, and the way we act at funerals, traces its way back down the chain to our worldview assumptions about life and death. As Hiebert has noted, worldview is not what we think about, but *what we think with.* Our worldview assumptions guide us in how we think about life. Cultural structures are coping mechanisms that are rooted in a people's worldview assumptions. Thus, worldview provides a framework for coping with life, for living effectively in one's social context.

Worldview as the Foundation of Culture

What all this adds up to is that a people's collective worldview assumptions serve as the foundation for their surface-level cultural structures and behaviors. The surface-level structures and behaviors are what we see. The deep-level assumptions are buried deep in the collective unconscious of the community and are not readily apparent. Just as the foundation of a building is part of the building, but is underneath and out of sight, so worldview is a part of a people's culture but is underneath and out of sight. Figure 5 illustrates how worldview serves as the underlying foundation upon which culture is constructed.

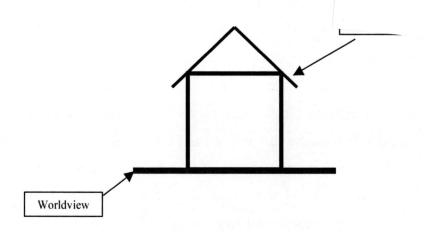

**FIGURE 5: WORLDVIEW AS THE
FOUNDATION OF CULTURE**

Given the role worldview plays in people's lives, it is clear
that if one wants to understand a group of people, if one wants to
know why those people are the way they are, understanding their
worldview is essential. It is absolutely crucial, therefore, that those
who teach in multicultural contexts (at any level) understand not
only the surface-level aspects of the cultures represented in their
classroom population, but the underlying assumptions of their
students as well.

Effective Multicultural Teacher Training

If teachers are to interact effectively with culturally-other students and teach ethnically diverse groups of students to be culturally aware, sensitive and tolerant, if they are to affirm different cultural perspectives and traditions, and at the same time prepare students for productive participation in American society (multicultural citizenship education), *it is essential that those teachers understand the worldview assumptions of the cultural groups represented in their classrooms.*

How can teachers gain the knowledge and skills necessary to understand the cultural assumptions of the ethnic groups they will be teaching? I suggest two basic features be integrated into the curriculum for teacher certification. First, during a teacher's undergraduate program at least two courses in cultural anthropology should be required. One should be Cultural Anthropology (not *Introduction to Anthropology*) and a second should be a Cultural Anthropology Seminar where students are required to do detailed research on the worldview assumptions and the subsequent cultural patterns of those ethnic groups that make up significant percentages of America's minority population, namely, Latino and Asian cultures.[10] Second, student teaching or

---

[10] Not all anthropology departments will offer courses that focus specifically on worldview as I have presented it in this chapter. Few, in fact, will. That is

practicum assignments should be completed in a context where non-Anglo students dominate the classroom population. During that practicum the student teacher should be required to continue cultural research in the form of extensive participant observation and a subsequent detailed ethnography of the ethnic group being studied.

Only with significant levels of anthropological course work, specific cultural research, and personal cross-cultural experience in the form of participant observation in/with another ethnic group will teachers gain the insights and skills necessary for effective cross-cultural interaction in the classroom and multicultural citizenship education that is appropriate and productive.

Summary

America is a multicultural society. The need for effective multicultural citizenship education exists today and will only become more pressing as we proceed through the early decades of

---

unfortunate and short sighted on their part. Discovering a people's deep-level underlying assumptions is time consuming and challenging work, requiring considerable qualitative research. Many anthropologists have failed to grasp the significance of these assumptions and have not therefore done the necessary research. However, prospective teachers, in taking standard cultural anthropology courses gain helpful insights into the underlying assumptions of the people of different ethnic identities. Understanding those underlying assumptions will lead to clearer insights as to why their surface-level culture is what it is.

the twenty-first century. Appropriate multicultural curriculum and teaching models are crucial. But even more crucial is teacher training that emphasizes appropriate anthropological training for educators, training that will allow them to develop an understanding of the importance of worldview assumptions of the various ethnic groups present in their classrooms.

This study of a philosophy of education in multicultural contexts involves three considerations: 1) the philosophy of education concern, 2) the multicultural concern, and 3) the philosophical paradigm concern. We have discussed the philosophy of education aspect: the goal of education is to produce moral citizens who can participate in meaningful, productive ways in society. The goal of education is citizenship education. We have also addressed the multicultural concern. To accomplish effective multicultural citizenship education teachers in multicultural contexts must be anthropologically informed and understand the worldviews and cultures of the students in their classrooms. Having discussed those two considerations, we are now confronted with the third concern of this study: a philosophical paradigm that will be help teachers accomplish their multicultural educational goals. That discussion will be the topic of Chapter 3.

CHAPTER 3

CRITICAL REALISM

As we have seen, philosophers and educators have long held that the goal of education is to prepare moral individuals for meaningful participation in society. The process, as we have noted, is referred to as *citizenship education*. To accomplish this goal in a multicultural context, educators need three things: 1) a clear vision of the process and the purposes, 2) thorough training not only in the subject matter they will teach but also in cultural anthropology and cross-cultural fieldwork so they can understand the culturally-other dynamic present in their classrooms, and 3) a philosophical paradigm that is specific enough to provide a framework for accomplishing the task but also flexible enough (or broad enough) to allow for creativity and dynamic development in a context that continues to evolve. This third concern is the subject of this chapter. Critical Realism is an appropriate philosophical paradigm that will allow educators to accomplish citizenship education in multicultural contexts.

To demonstrate how Critical Realism is an appropriate paradigm for accomplishing citizenship education in multicultural contexts will require 1) a discussion of paradigms and their importance, 2) a definition of Critical Realism, and 3) a discussion of how Critical Realism is particularly well suited for accomplishing citizenship education in multicultural contexts. From this point forward in the discussion I will refer to Critical Realism simply as CR.

The Function of Paradigms

What is a paradigm and why do educators, especially those who teach in multicultural contexts, need one? Generally speaking, a paradigm is a set of assumptions, perspectives, and concepts that provide a framework or structure for thinking, interpreting, and doing what one does within a given discipline. A scientific paradigm, for example, provides scientists with a flexible framework for observing and scrutinizing, formulating questions, designing experiments, and interpreting data.[11] Fo

philosophical paradigm provides a flexible conce

for essential functioning including: 1) conceptualizing the specific

process (citizenship education in a multicultural context), 2)

identifying general and specific goals (age appropriate academic

curriculum as well as ethnic inclusive and affirming curriculum),

3) analyzing the physical, emotive, and rational context (for

example an overcrowded, ethnically and socioeconomically

diverse fourth grade classroom) in which multicultural educational

goals are accomplished, 4) designing creative projects and

exercises for accomplishing the goals, and 5) designing creative

methods for measuring their own (the teacher's) progress as well

as that of their students. I suggest that CR is an appropriate

paradigm for accomplishing these aspects of the educational

process.

We often talk about creative, alternative thinking as

"thinking outside the box." Occasionally, such thinking is

necessary and helpful. On a day-to-day basis, however, it is the

box that provides structure and stability. We know what to do,

how to do it, and what to expect from others because the *box* is

---

[11] In his 1962 book, *The Structures of Scientific Revolutions*, Thomas Kuhn
wrote about how scientific paradigms shift dramatically in revolutionary ways, a
completely new paradigm replacing an old one, usually as a new generation of
scientists begin to approach their fields from new perspectives.

there, providing a framework (hopefully a flexible one) for thinking and acting. The *box* is a paradigm. Thinking outside the box occasionally is a good and necessary thing. But without the *box* life would be undirected and unfocused. It would be chaotic. Paradigms are essential for effective functioning in a complex world.

Paradigms are most effective when they are identifiable and intentional. Most professional people have some sort of a paradigm from which they work. For some it may be nothing more than a vague set of ideas that provide some basic parameters. However, the more challenging and complex a task is, the more important an intentional well-defined paradigm becomes. Citizenship education in a multicultural context is so challenging and complex that an intentional and well-defined paradigm from which to work in accomplishing the task is essential. CR is such a paradigm. Before discussing CR in detail, however, it is necessary to clarify some terminology.

Clarifying Terminology

To understand CR it is necessary to contrast it with Idealism and Realism. It is also necessary to distinguish between different forms of CR advocated by philosophers past and present.

Idealism

Idealism, in its most basic sense, suggests that reality is fundamentally mental rather than material in nature (Blackburn 184; Crane 26). Idealism is the view "that the real objects constituting the 'external world' are not independent of cognizing minds, but exist only as in some way correlative to mental operations... the conception that reality as we understand it reflects the workings of the mind" (Rescher 412-413). Berkeley said, "no object exists apart from the mind; mind is therefore the deepest reality" (Crane 29).

To say that REALITY is mediated by the mental, that the mind interprets REALITY so that one person experiences and interprets REALITY differently from another person, is a defensible position. To suggest that an external REALITY separate from the mind perceiving it does not exist is, in my opinion, indefensible. This, however, is what idealism suggests, that an external REALITY apart from what the mind perceives does not exist.

As odd as Idealism may sound to people who are the intellectual products of the late twentieth century, at the close of the nineteenth century Idealism was the dominant epistemological paradigm for understanding reality (Hirst 77). Rescher helps us understand why:

> Perhaps the strongest argument favoring idealism is that any characterization of the real that we can devise is bound to be a mind-constructed one: our only access to information about what the real is is through the mediation of mind. What seems right about idealism is inherent in the fact that in investigating the real we are clearly constrained to use our own concepts to address our own issues—that we learn about the real only in our own terms of reference. (413)

Rescher is right in pointing out the mind-dependent nature of all perception. Perception occurs in the mind. Different minds may perceive the same REALITY differently. The issue, however, with which I am concerned in considering Idealism and the subsequent development of Realism is not whether or not perception is mind-dependent, but whether or not an objective REALITY exists separate from the minds that perceive it. If a tree falls in the woods and no one is there to hear (perceive) the noise it makes, does it make noise?[12]

---

[12] Some philosophers might object that 19th century Idealists, such as Berkeley, believed in a real world and that to suggest that they did not is to fail to understand Idealism. That criticism is accurate, but only to a degree. Berkeley acknowledged that "things" exist apart from his perception of them, but that they still exist only as they are perceived. Berkeley avoided a contradictory dilemma by suggesting that the mind that conceives the world is God's mind. God, perceiving the world in his mind, makes it real for the rest of us. Of course we are still left with a serious question: if the world only exists in God's mind, does it really exist? Is there an objective world that exists apart from the divine mind? Definitional challenges aside, in a time of a rapidly evolving scientific enterprise (the 19th century), a paradigm from which to conduct scientific research that was less subjective and more objective was considered essential. Realism, therefore, as a more scientific-friendly philosophical paradigm developed in contrast to Idealism, providing greater objectivity for the scientific enterprise.

71

While Idealism as a philosophical perspective has been disregarded by most people in favor Realism (defined below), it must be admitted that nineteenth century Idealists were, to a degree, aware of an important truth—that the perception of REALITY is mind-dependent. There is a difference, however, between REALITY and our perception of it. The problem with Idealism, especially in terms of scientific investigation, is that if the world exists only as it is perceived in the mind, what is the point of expending time, effort, and resources in critical analysis of the physical world? If Idealism is correct, it might be concluded that reality is nothing more than what an individual perceives it to be.[13] As the West deepened its interest in the sciences during the later part of the 19th century, the limitations of Idealism and the need for a more scientifically friendly epistemological paradigm became apparent. Idealism gave way to Realism.

Realism

Realism is "the view that material objects exist externally to us and independently of our sense experience" (Hirst 77 Vol. 7).

---

[13] Even if this conclusion regarding the end result of an Idealistic perspective as I have explained it is incorrect, the historical reality is that Idealism was abandoned in favor of Realism, which happens to advocate an objective reality that exists separate from perceiving minds. If a tree falls in the forest and no one is there to hear it (perceive it), does it make a noise? A Realist would say, yes.

This is obviously a very broad definition, leaving room for different views and expressions of the idea. One form of Realism that must be noted is Direct Realism. Direct Realism suggests that REALITY is experienced in a direct, unmediated way, that one's experience or perception of REALITY represents REALITY exactly as it really is (Heil 237). Just as a photograph of a person looks just like that person, one's perception of REALITY is what REALITY really looks like. Direct Realism advocates a position that is basically the opposite of Idealism, completely ignoring the role of the observer in the process of observation. It may be that few (if any) philosophers ever embraced Direct Realism, but the average person, including many educators, assumes that their perception is direct.

Direct Realism is also sometimes called Naïve Realism—for obvious reasons. The difficulties associated with it were not lost on those thinking critically about REALITY and the human perception of it. That a real world that exists separate from human perception of it appeared to be obvious. It also appeared obvious that our perception of REALITY is impacted in various ways by several things: culture, gender, age, and education to name a few.[14]

---

[14] A husband and wife attending the same party may have different interpretations (perspectives) of conversations that took place at the party. Men often see things one way and women see them another. Why? Because gender/sex impact one's perception of what is happening, that is, of REALITY.

Direct Realism as a paradigm for thinking about REALITY and interpreting scientific data is flawed. It denies or ignores the individual subjective nature of perception. Idealism, however, was just as flawed. It had gone so far in the other direction emphasizing subjectivity that for all practical purposes any measure of objectivity was eliminated. Something between the two extremes (between Idealism and Direct Realism) was needed. Realism, in its simplest expression is "the view that material objects exist externally to us and independently of our sense experience" was too broad a realization to provide a functional paradigm. It served as an alternative to Idealism, but was not specific enough to be a useful paradigm. This is where CR comes into play.

Critical Realism

Generally speaking, CR is a philosophical paradigm "that acknowledges the mediation of 'the mental' in our cognitive grasp of the physical world" (Delaney 194). CR stands half way between Idealism and Realism in that it acknowledges that a real

---

So do age, education, past experiences, and most importantly, one's culture. Perception is not direct and exact. If it were, people witnessing the same events would always see it exactly the same way. But they do not. Ask witnesses of an accident to tell you what they saw and the descriptions will vary from person to person. Why? Because perception is subjective.

external world exists separate from human perception of it, but that the real world must be perceived by means of the mental, which amounts to a subjective mental experience of real world.[15]

Acknowledging the existence of a real world that can be studied and understood is highly significant, the implications considerable. A real world that can be studied and understood implies an objective REALITY. The laws of physics are part of an objective REALITY. Gravity, for instance, is an objective REALITY. Understanding gravity in a given cultural context may

---

[15] CR can be traced back to Charles Peirce in 1877. In a 1905 article he referred to it as *Critical Common-Sensism*. Between 1916-1920, Sellas and others reintroduced the idea. More recently, Roy Bhaskar (*Critical Realism: Essential Readings*) has brought CR to the fore as part of the discussion related to the Philosophy of Science. A number of philosophers interested in the social sciences (Cruickshank et. al. *Critical Realism: The Difference it Makes*, and Jose Lopez and Garry Potter, *After Postmodernism: An Introduction to Critical Realism*) following Bhaskar have embraced CR in response to some of the challenges of postmodern theory. These philosophers take CR in a slightly different direction than I do in this study. My use of CR has to do with the original development of the concept. The *realism* aspect of CR acknowledges a real world external to and independent of human perception of it. The *critical* aspect of CR acknowledges that perception of the real external world occurs in the mind and is therefore a subjective experience. An objective REALITY exists and can be studied and contemplated. Truths can be discovered. But REALITY is perceived and truths discovered in the context in which the perceiving, discovering minds exist, that is, in cultural contexts. REALITY can be said to be objective in the sense that it exists apart from human perception of it, but human minds can only perceive REALITY subjectively. There are, however, certain aspects of REALITY that transcend the subjective nature of human perception. In a base ten system, two plus two equals four regardless of contextual concerns that might impact subjective perception, such as cultural context. Thus, the importance of CR as a paradigm that stresses both the objective nature of REALITY and the [mostly] subjective perception of it.

be a subjective, mind-dependent experience (the specific word for gravity, the way the phenomenon is explained, especially in a culture that is not scientifically oriented), but gravity as a physical phenomenon is an objective REALITY that transcends cultural and perceptual contexts. And because there is an objective reality, even though it is subjectively understood or experienced, that objective REALITY can be studied and understood.

The American philosopher Charles S. Peirce discussed this idea in an article he wrote in 1877:

> There are Real things, whose characters are entirely independent of our opinions about them; those Reals affect our senses according to regular laws, and, though our sensations are as different as our relations to the objects, yet, by taking advantage of the laws of perception, we can ascertain by reasoning how things really and truly are; and any man, if he have sufficient experience and he reason enough about it, will be led to the one True conclusion. (Buchler 18)

Peirce affirmed that objective REALITY can be ascertained. Is this true only for material substances where empirical verification is possible? Or does the ascertaining of an objective REALITY extend to the realm of ideas as well? Socrates, Plato, and Aristotle, followed by a host of other philosophers, would say yes. Ideas, concepts, principles—things that can be mathematically or logically evaluated—are also part of objective REALITY. They are things that can be rationally verified. Empirically available or rationally available, objective

REALITY, even though it is subjectively perceived, is not diminished by the subjectivity of the perception.

The *realism* part of CR has to do with an objective REALITY that can be ascertained. The *critical* part of CR has to do with the subjective experience of REALITY. What is the basis of one's subjective mental experience of REALITY? What shapes the experience? It is one's cultural context, one's worldview assumptions. Other factors that will impact one's experience of REALITY include age, gender, and previous experiences. However, the key factor, and the focus of this study, is the impact culture has on one's experience of REALITY.

The connection between CR and culture and therefore of a paradigm for a philosophy of education in multicultural contexts may not, at first, be apparent. However, since CR acknowledges that the perception of REALITY is mind dependent, and since it is in the enculturation process that the mind learns to do what it does in culturally appropriate ways (for instance, one's language provides categories for thought), then it is clear that *that which is mind-dependent is also culture-dependent.* If CR stresses the role of the mind in the perception of REALITY then it also stresses the role of culture in the perception of REALITY. The way we perceive the world we live in depends a great deal on the culture in

77

which we were enculturated. That fact makes the whole issue central to multicultural education.

Two additional terms need clarifying before we move on to a more detailed discussion of CR as a paradigm for accomplishing citizenship education in multicultural contexts. They are *acculturation* and *assimilation*.

Acculturation

Acculturation is the process of learning a second culture. Enculturation is the process of acquiring one's primary culture. Enculturation occurs throughout childhood as we learn our language and develop evaluative, emotive, and cognitive responses and processes appropriate for our cultural context. Learning how to function in a second culture is the process of *acculturation*. It involves learning the language and the surface-level cultural patterns of the new cultural context in which one lives (Rogers 37-43).

Assimilation

Assimilation is the intentional embracing and integration/absorption into a secondary culture. While acculturation creates functionality in a second culture (learning the language and the surface-level cultural patterns) assimilation goes deeper and represents the desire to embrace the new culture, allowing old perspectives and habits to be replaced by new ones. Assimilation involves a significant change in personality, for it requires the development of new worldview assumptions and new culturally appropriate ways of thinking, feeling, and responding (Rogers 43-46).

Acculturation and assimilation are extremely important concepts in multicultural education. They have to do with the appropriate expectations of the dominant culture. Is it enough for students to acculturate? Or must they be required to assimilate (as defined above)? Does effective citizenship education demand assimilation? Or can the goals of citizenship education be accomplished with or in students who accept acculturation but who do not fully embrace assimilation? Put another way, can a culturally-other person who does not desire to be assimilated into the mainstream dominant culture participate in a moral, meaningful way (as defined in Chapter 1) in American society? These questions and concerns are foundational to effective citizenship education in multicultural contexts. My contention is that CR is a philosophical paradigm that allows such questions to be addressed effectively and it is, therefore, especially helpful and appropriate as a paradigm for citizenship education in multicultural contexts.

At this point it is necessary to go a little deeper into CR, discussing what it offers in the way of an effective paradigm for citizenship education in multicultural contexts.

REALITY from a Critical Realism Perspective

The world exists independent of the minds that perceive it. I have been referring to that real world as REALITY. What does that REALITY include? For me, it includes all that really exists materially and spiritually, including God and the moral absolutes that inevitably flow from his nature.[16] Earlier I quoted Hirst who spoke of Realism as referring to "material objects." Obviously, I am expanding the definition of REALITY from only the material (or physical) to also include the metaphysical as well. That fact that a thing is not material does mean that it is not real. The metaphysical is just as real as the physical and is rightfully included in a discussion of CR as an appropriate paradigm for the philosophy of education. This is a basic assumption of this study. The point in the context of this study is that from the perspective of

---

[16] CR does not require a dualist perspective or belief in God, but certainly allows for it as long as one acknowledges the mind-dependent nature of perceiving REALITY. Two prominent Christian anthropologists have written texts (Charles H. Kraft, *Anthropology for Christian Witness*, and Paul G. Hiebert, *Missiological Implications of Epistemological Shifts*) proposing CR as a philosophical paradigm appropriate for a Christian perspective on REALITY. There is nothing about CR as a philosophical paradigm that is inherently materialistic.

CR, objective REALITY exists and is experienced by people who make sense of it (interpret it and respond to it) as it is filtered through their worldview. As noted earlier, since our underlying assumptions about REALITY are acquired in the enculturation process, how one experiences and interprets REALITY depends on the cultural context in which one grew up.

It is crucial to keep in mind that the *realism* aspect of CR focuses on the existence of an objective REALITY that exists separate from how it is perceived. The *critical* aspect of CR focuses on the subjective perception of that objective REALITY. The subjective perception of an objective REALITY may at first appear contradictory. It is not. In some cases the subjective aspect is minimal. For instance, in Mexico and in Mongolia, 2+2=4. The languages used to express the equation may be different, but the perception of the REALITY is the same in either context. The logical precision of mathematics, however, is not available for every consideration. For instance, while and teaching college in Nigeria, West Africa it became apparent to me that Nigerian people experienced some aspects of REALITY differently than I did. They had different worldview assumptions and thought differently and responded differently to some things than I did.

Living in close proximity (the students lived in campus dorms, faculty lived in campus housing) we experienced the same

REALITY: sickness (malaria), poverty, fatigue, worry, joy, hope, death, birth, opposition, heat, cold, hunger, thirst, fear, disappointment, laughter, friendship, confusion, discovery, insight, accomplishment, failure: all the aspects of living life in a real world. Though we experienced the same REALITY, we interpreted much of it differently. Their interpretation of and response to REALITY grew out of different assumptions regarding causes and appropriate responses to things that occurred. Different assumptions about REALITY led to different conclusions about REALITY.

How do these different assumptions and conclusions manifest themselves in practical, social ways? One day in class a student said to me, "The Bible says not to kill, does it not?" I replied that it did. He then said, "We have heard that in America you can kill someone and not go to jail. Is that right?" I thought for a moment before answering. "Well," I said, "our laws make provision for defending yourself. If someone is trying to hurt or kill you, you have the right to defend yourself. If, in the process of defending yourself, you kill your attacker, you will not be charged with a crime." My students were astonished. "In Nigeria," they explained, "if you kill someone, no matter the reason, you go to jail. Killing is wrong." Obviously they do not distinguish, as we do, between different forms and motives/purposes involved in the ending of a life. In the West we recognize that it is possible to "kill" someone without murdering them. Soldiers and police kill people in the line of duty. That does not make them murderers. Killing someone in self-defense does not make one a murderer. The Nigerians had a different perspective on *taking life* than I did. Their perception (interpretation) of REALITY was different from mine.

In that exchange, we were experiencing what was for them a theological conundrum. I was their teacher and they respected me. But as an American theologian I was espousing a moral position they believed to be very wrong. We shared a number of beliefs about God and the Bible, about faith and Christian living. But on this moral issue we differed dramatically. Who was right?

Individuals working out of a Naïve Realism perspective (and many Americans not trained in philosophy do—including many theologians) would assume that since they see things the way they really are, that their perspective on self-defense is correct. Most Nigerians work out of a Naïve Realism perspective and believe their point of view represents *the* objective, accurate, truth of the issue under consideration—in this case the taking of a life in self-defense. Individuals on the opposite end of the philosophical spectrum from Naïve Realism, those who espouse absolute relativity,[17] would suggest that there are no moral absolutes. For the absolute relativist, each perspective on the taking of a life in self-defense, the American perspective and the Nigerian perspective, is right for each group in their respective cultural contexts. Their concern would be that neither side seems to understand that everything is relative.

I suggest that neither Naïve Realism nor absolute relativity provide an acceptable paradigm for thinking about social and moral concerns. Each represents an extreme position. CR provides a middle ground between the two. CR allows for the possibility that REALITY includes the existence of God and the moral absolutes that flow from his nature. As noted, a prohibition against murder is one of those absolutes. However, since according to CR, the perception of REALITY is mind-dependent and therefore also culture-dependent, we must allow for different interpretations of REALITY. We must be culturally sensitive to and respectful of different views without slipping into the abyss of absolute relativity. CR provides a philosophical paradigm that recognizes the appropriateness of *relative cultural relativity*

---

[17] Some might question whether or not there are, in fact, any people who actually espouse absolute relativity. There may be only a few philosophers who embrace the idea but there are some. Also, among the general population, which includes many educators, the idea appears to be quite popular. Admittedly, many will abandon the idea of *absolute* relativity after considering a few basic objections.

(defined in footnote # 18 in the next section) and the cultural sensitivity and respect that go with it. CR also avoids the challenges of paradigms that result in absolute relativity because they do not recognize moral absolutes as an aspect of REALITY.

What does all this have to do with philosophy of education in multicultural contexts? The educational environment in American schools today includes a vast mosaic of ethnicities and worldviews, value systems and cultural patterns. Teachers do what they do in an intensely pluralistic context. They need a philosophical paradigm from which to approach their task that will: 1) provide them with a framework for teaching a curriculum designed to prepare students for meaningful participation in an ethnically diverse democratic society, and 2) that will enable them to accomplish that goal in culturally sensitive, inclusive ways. In the following section I will demonstrate how and why CR is a paradigm that meet both of those needs.

Critical Realism and Multicultural Education

Why is CR an appropriate paradigm for a philosophy of education in multicultural contexts? There are four reasons.

First, CR is appropriate for effective education in multicultural contexts because it is a framework that requires the embracing of *relative* cultural relativism without going to the extreme of *absolute* cultural relativism.[18]   As noted above, CR allows for a REALITY that includes God and, therefore, the moral absolutes that flow from his nature. Even if one does not believe in the existence of God, but sees the necessity of having a moral system that is not rooted in absolute cultural relativity, CR works effectively. It does not require belief in God, but allows for belief if that is part of one's assumptions regarding REALITY.

What does this have to do with citizenship education in multicultural contexts? It is important because of the goals of citizenship education.   As noted in Chapter 1, the Greek philosophers believed that a moral person was one focused on the pursuit of inner excellence. For them, a moral person was a happy, thriving person, fulfilling his purpose in life. This was considered a virtuous life. They believed that education ought to prepare a

---

[18] The difference between *relative* cultural relativity and *absolute* cultural relativity is considerable and significant. R. W Hepburn notes that according to ethical relativism (what I am referring to as absolute cultural relativity) "…moral appraisals are essentially dependent upon the standards that define a particular moral code, the practices and norms accepted by a social group at a specific place and time. Given that there is in fact a plurality of social groups, with differing mores, the relativist argues that there exist no point of view from which these codes can themselves be appraised, no 'absolute' criteria by which they can be criticized" (800). In other words, no moral absolutes exist. In contrast, *relative* cultural relativity suggests that while different cultures have considerable leeway in determining acceptable and unacceptable behavior in their society, moral absolutes exist and are the ultimate determinants of right and wrong. The challenge, of course, even when the concept of moral absolutes is accepted, is in determining what is included in the list. That discussion, however, is beyond the scope of this study.

person for that kind of life, a life of meaningful participation in society, reaching one's full potential as a person, and thereby contributing constructively to the social community of which one is a citizen. Many philosophers and educators through the centuries, including many contemporary philosophers of education, maintain essentially the same goals for education.

Philosophical paradigms that result in absolute cultural relativity cannot provide students with the foundation necessary for meaningful and just participation in a society where moral citizenship is the goal not only in that specific society but also in a complex culturally diverse global community. Absolute relativity results in conclusions and behaviors that are simply unacceptable. An old but effective illustration of the dangers of absolute relativity is the Nazi response to the Jews in their society. The Nazis believed the Jews presented a threat to their way of life, that is, to their cultural context. Their response to the perceived threat was to eliminate the threat by means of ethnic genocide. Jews were exterminated as if they were rodents or insects. The idea of absolute cultural relativity suggests that since the Nazis (the dominant force in German culture at that time) concluded that "their" culture[19] was threatened by the presence of the Jews and

---

[19] Whether it was actually their culture or not is irrelevant to the point being made.

that they were simply responding to the threat in a way they considered appropriate, no one outside their culture had a right to suggest that the course of action they chose to respond to the threat was inappropriate. However, other nations did suggest that their response was inappropriate. Ethnic genocide was not appropriate, not acceptable. Why not? The reason given was the existence of a *higher moral law* that makes such behavior unacceptable. But what did that mean? Was the *higher moral law* rooted in the majority opinion of the collective nations that prosecuted the Nazis? Was it *higher* because more people were against ethnic genocide than were for it? Or was there actually a higher moral law (a law that transcended all human thinking and culture) that made ethnic genocide wrong regardless of what any group of people, large or small, thought about it? Why was ethnic genocide wrong? Because people said it was? Or because it really was morally wrong? To say that it really was morally wrong is to acknowledge the existence of moral absolutes and deny the validity of absolute cultural relativity.

The female infanticide that occurred in China during (and after) the cultural revolution is another example of how absolute relativity results in behavior that is simply unacceptable. Chinese families were allowed to have only one child. Families that had a second child were subject to severe economic sanctions. Since their social system placed a premium on male children (male children in China are responsible for caring for elderly parents), if a couple had a daughter instead of a son, the infant girl was often killed or left to die so they could try again, hoping for a son. In their cultural context this was perfectly acceptable—absolute cultural relativity. But is female infanticide for any reason in any context ever acceptable? If it is not, then a philosophical system (paradigm) that leads to such conclusions and behaviors is not acceptable either.

The whole issue of human rights, which is of primary importance in Western societies, along with their international interests and influences, is a testimony to the reality of a higher moral law that determines the ultimate rightness or wrongness of how one group of humans treats another group of humans. The Declaration of Independence says, *"We hold these truths to be self-evident, that all men are created equal, that they are endowed by their Creator with certain unalienable Rights, that among these are Life, Liberty and the pursuit of Happiness."* These *unalienable rights*, the founding fathers recognized, are rights that transcend culture. All people are endowed with these rights and they are clear evidence of a moral law (moral imperatives) that transcend human will and culture. They exist whether or not humans recognize them.[20]   Whatever else might be involved in a philosophy of education, a focus on basic human rights and dignity must be part of it. Philosophical paradigms that lead to absolute relativity and the brutality that can be part of those systems are unacceptable frameworks for citizenship education in a multicultural society that is part of a complex and diverse global community. An *"anything is acceptable as long as enough people say it is"* philosophy is not an appropriate framework for a moral society and certainly does not provide an appropriate philosophical paradigm for citizenship education.

CR allows one to avoid the unacceptable extremes of absolute relativity by allowing for a view of REALITY that includes moral absolutes. CR advocates relative cultural relativity (which demonstrates respect for other cultures), but allows for the teaching and practice of moral absolutes in a way that is philosophically consistent and culturally appropriate for citizenship in a multicultural, pluralistic society. How does it do this? What

---

[20] In, *Ethics: Approaching Moral Decisions*, Arthur F. Holmes provides an excellent discussion of the ethics of human rights, suggesting that a Christian perspective provides a superior bases for human rights (83-94). It is important to note, however, that it is not necessary to espouse a Christian perspective to uphold human rights as transcendent of human will and culture. A humanistic perspective on the intrinsic value of the human being results in the same basic perspective (for different reasons, granted, but the same basic perspective nonetheless) of a moral imperative regarding the proper view and treatment of each human being. Moral absolutes beyond human will and culture exist.

is the link between CR and moral absolutes? CR acknowledges that an objective REALITY exists and can be ascertained. Such an ascertainable objective REALITY includes not only material substances subject to empirical verification, but also rational truths subject to logical verification, truths or concepts such as $2 + 2 = 4$, and propositional truths such as: *Something cannot come from nothing. If something exists now, then something has always existed. Something exists now. Therefore something has always existed.* As Peirce said, "we can ascertain by reasoning how things really and truly are; and any man, if he have sufficient experience and he reason enough about it, will be led to the one True conclusion" (Buchler 18). Such reasoning about the nature of life quickly leads into a discussion of good and evil, of right and wrong, of whether or not there are moral absolutes and if so what they might be. CR is linked to moral absolutes in that it is open to the ascertaining of an objective REALITY, empirically and rationally. CR, therefore, is an appropriate paradigm for accomplishing citizenship education in multicultural contexts, for students from diverse cultural contexts need to be introduced to and instructed in the rational foundations of virtuous citizenship, foundations rooted in moral absolutes as well as in the social norms of contemporary society.

Second, CR is appropriate for citizenship education in multicultural contexts because on the *critical* side of CR it acknowledges that REALITY is culturally perceived, interpreted, and lived, thereby requiring educators to be culturally aware, sensitive, and respectful. Moral absolutes are part of REALITY. But since all REALITY is mediated by means of mental processes, and since mental processes are structured according to one's worldview assumptions, and since worldview assumptions are determined by one's cultural context, then REALITY and the moral absolutes that are part of it are culturally mediated.[21] REALITY is culturally perceived and interpreted, but moral imperatives that transcend the relativity of cultural perception exist. They are above culture, or are *supracultural.*[22] These supracultural imperatives (for example, the wrongness of genocide,

---

[21] Moral absolutes being culturally mediated means that moral absolutes are culturally interpreted and applied, but absolutes still exist and must be acknowledged in some way. Americans may not interpret and apply prohibitions against killing the same way Nigerians do, but both Americans and Nigerians acknowledge that there are absolutes regarding the sanctity of human life.

[22] There are mathematical concepts that are universal or supracultural. $2+2=4$ in every cultural context. Logical principles are also supracultural. That a thing cannot both exist and not exist at the same time is true in every cultural context. Just as there are mathematical and logical principles that are supracultural, there are moral imperatives (such as the evil of ethnocide) that are supracultural. Ethnocide is evil everywhere, all the time, not because the majority says it is, but because human life has intrinsic value that must be respected.

the rightness of human rights) exist as part of REALITY that must be recognized and incorporated into cultural awareness and patterns of behavior, becoming *reality* for the people of a given society.[23]

Are there other ways the *critical* aspect of CR enhances multicultural education? Yes. Different perceptions of REALITY must be recognized and respected in multicultural educational contexts. That recognition is important whether it involves concerns related to human rights, appropriate ways of recognizing and respecting authority, or appropriate ways of dressing. For example, in a multicultural educational context, failure to recognize the validity and value of cultural patterns other than those of the dominant culture is disrespectful and demeaning. It can also lead to unnecessary conflict and emotional trauma for students. In some Asian cultures, for instance, it is disrespectful to make eye contact with authority figures, which for children and students would include teachers. Yet in an Anglo context the expected behavior is just the opposite: making eye contact is a sign of respect. Not doing so can be considered disrespectful. Teachers who might require Asian students to make eye contact ("look at me

---

[23] That the people of a given culture may not recognize a given moral imperative does not impact the existence of the moral imperative. A child may not recognize that 2+2=4. That does not mean, however, that 2+2 does not equal 4.

when I'm talking to you") create unnecessary conflict within culturally-other students. Dozens of other examples would serve to illustrate the same point: cultural awareness is essential for teaching in multicultural contexts.

While it is certainly possible for teachers to become culturally aware and sensitive without embracing CR as part of their philosophy of education, working out of a paradigm that stresses the importance of cultural awareness makes it more likely that the desired result will be achieved to a more significant level.

Third, CR is an appropriate paradigm for citizenship education in multicultural contexts because by acknowledging that REALITY is culturally perceived, CR results in realistic expectations regarding acculturation and assimilation. In the present context of American multicultural education, educators who embrace an *assimilationist* perspective propose that educational processes ought to lend themselves to the ultimate goal of assimilation into the mainstream dominant culture (Williams 25-32; Green and Perlman 317-326). One of the problems of the assimilationist position is a basic misunderstanding of the differences between *acculturation* and *assimilation* and the significant challenges related to assimilation for generation 1 and

1.5 immigrants.[24]   What is the difference between acculturation and assimilation and what can reasonably be expected from culturally-other students who make up a significant portion of the contemporary student population?[25]

As noted earlier, acculturation is the process of learning a second culture. It is a complicated, time consuming process. As children, we *absorb* our culture as it is *transmitted* to us more than we learn it in any intentional way as it is taught to us. Even before we are born we hear our parent's voices speaking the language that will become our own. As babies, we experience our world through sensory encounters: sights, sounds, smells, textures, tastes, and so forth that we do not fully comprehend. As toddlers we begin to explore, to experience, to absorb. During our first few years of life, as we learn our language, we learn (unconsciously, and some learn better than others) the thought patterns and processes required to function in our culture. All the things we experience transmit to us something about the world in which we live—our

---

[24] A generation 1 immigrant is an immigrant who was fully enculturated in his or her home culture before immigrating to another culture. A generation1.5 immigrant is a child or young person (a child between the ages of 6 and 12 for example, though no exact age limits may be set) who was partially but not fully enculturated in his or her home culture before being brought to another culture by his or her family.

[25] The following material on assimilation and acculturation is taken from *Evangelizing Immigrants*, Rogers, 2006.

cultural context.   As children, we do not analyze what we experience.   For the most part, we simply absorb and accept it. Though many children go through a phase of asking "why," we accept most of what we learn (experience) without thinking about it.

Enculturation is, on our part, an unintentional act.   Our parents, siblings and teachers intentionally instruct us, but seldom with the specific intent of teaching us our culture.   That is why it is more accurate to speak of our culture being *transmitted* to us more than being *taught* to us. However, when it comes to learning a second culture (acculturation), it is necessary to be intentional.

Children who immigrate (normally with their parents) at say eight or ten years old have been enculturated to a significant degree in their home culture.   They, like their parents, must now be acculturated, that is, they must learn a new culture.   But because they are still children, they are still in what might be called an *active learning mode*.   They learn (absorb) things quite easily. They will learn their new culture much more easily than their parents who no longer learn as easily as they once did. Acculturation for young people (generation 1.5s) must be more intentional than their enculturation had been, but it will require less effort and less time than will be required for adults.   Acculturation for adults (generation 1 immigrants) must be intentional and will be a slower process.

In the simplest terms, culture learning occurs on two levels: the surface-level and the deep-level. Learning the surface-level features of a new culture is easier than learning the deep-level features. This is not to say that surface-level acculturation is easy. It is not. But compared to deep-level culture learning, surface-level is easier. What are the surface-level features of culture that immigrants must learn in the process of acculturation? To answer this question we must first think about what culture is and how it is constructed.

First, culture is an *integrated whole*. Different parts of culture can be analyzed and discussed, but all parts of culture are interconnected. Second, culture is a *system*. The integrated parts work together to form a unified whole. Third, culture is *learned*, or as noted, it is transmitted and absorbed as children grow. Fourth, culture is *patterns of behaviors, ideas and products*. Culture is the way a people act, the way they think, the things they make. Culture is everything about a group of people.

As discussed in Chapter 2, culture is a three-tiered phenomenon made up 1) of our *deep-level* assumptions about REALITY, that is, about the world and about how life is to be lived (*worldview*), 2) of our *mid-level* internal responses—values

97

and our ways of feeling and thinking that grow out of our deep-level worldview assumptions, and 3) of our *surface-level* behaviors and structures. Figure 6 illustrates this three-tiered view of culture.

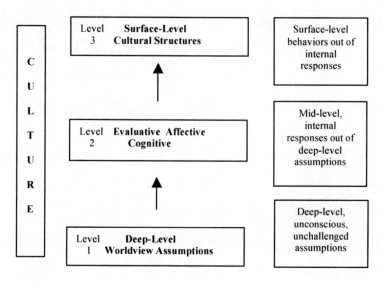

FIGURE 6: THREE-TIERED VIEW OF CULTURE

Think of culture as the house you live in. Our deep-level worldview assumptions about the world and how to live life serve as the foundation of your house. The house is then built on the foundation. Inside the walls of the building are the pipes, wires, conduit and ducting that make the house safe, comfortable and functional. The foundation and the stuff inside the walls remain mostly out of sight. What we think of as our house are the parts

98

we see and touch: the exterior walls and interior partitioning, the parts that are, for all practical purposes, the house we live in.

Our deep-level worldview assumptions about life can be compared to the foundation of the house. Our internal values, feelings and thinking are the pipes and wires in the walls. The way our culture is lived in everyday life is like the exterior and interior walls of the house. The foundation, pipes and wires are part of the house just as surely as are the walls, but because we don't see them we tend to forget them.

When you go to buy a house, the first thing you do when the real estate agent drives you up to the house, is look at the house—the outside of the house, the part visible from the street. When you go inside you take a quick look around to get a feel for the place. Then, if you are interested, you begin looking more closely.

The process of surface-level acculturation is like looking at the parts of the house that are visible, the parts easily seen and examined. Surface-level culture (level 3) is comprised of the behaviors and structures of a group of people. What kinds of things are these? Cultural structures are the frameworks we develop and use to accomplish the important activities of our society. Our educational system is a cultural structure, as is our political system. Our economic system (capitalism) is a cultural structure, as is our medical system. The various forms of religious expressions present in our society are cultural structures in that they allow us to express our faith in culturally appropriate ways. Our legal system is a cultural structure, as are our systems of transportation, our ways of structuring our families, our options for entertainment and recreation, our ways of celebrating or coping with the important events of life: births, weddings, deaths and so forth. These and other cultural structures allow us, as a cohesive society, to live out our lives in a meaningful, orderly, and for the most part, effective manner.

Cultural structures provide a framework for the way we do things (behaviors) as we live our lives. If our educational system is a *cultural structure*, going to school is a *cultural behavior*. If democracy is one of our cultural structures, then voting is one of our cultural behaviors. Everything we do is a cultural behavior because all of our behaviors are carried out within the context of our culture. We do what we do the way our culture tells us to do it. We behave in culturally appropriate ways.

When we go out to eat in a restaurant, unless we are intending to enjoy a unique and culturally-different experience, we sit on chairs and use silverware. To do so is, for us, culturally appropriate. In some cultures, going out to a restaurant would involve sitting on pillows on the floor and eating with one's right hand, primarily with the first and second fingers and the thumb.

Our cultural structures tell us what side of the road to drive on and when to stop and when to go. Our cultural structures tell us what parts of our bodies need to be covered in public, how to greet people, how to go shopping, how to build our houses and how to arrange for sleeping and other activities in our houses. Our culture, through our unique set of linguistic symbols (including the rules for using those symbols) provides a means for communicating effectively with others who share our culture. Our culture provides a framework (guidelines) for appropriate behavior.

Surface-level cultural structures and behaviors (level 3 of our three-tiered cultural construct) are the ways we live out our ideas and assumptions about how life should be lived. These surface-level structures and behaviors are the first things people new to our culture must learn if they are to survive here.

Surface-level culture learning is not as simple as some might assume. Depending on what culture immigrants might come from, our surface-level structures and behaviors might be very different from those of their home culture. Immigrants need to learn our cultural ways: how to communicate, how to shop, how to send their children to school, how to take their children to the

doctor, how to get a driver's license, how to find a pl
how to have their utilities turned on, how to open a bank account,
how to keep their immigration paperwork current, how to find and
keep a job. They need to learn about weddings and funerals, about
voting and about going to the library, about getting along with
neighbors, about hot dogs, apple pie and baseball, and about all the
new opportunities that await them in this amazing place called
America.

As challenging as surface-level culture learning can be,
deep-level cultural learning is even more challenging. The reason
for this is simple: surface-level culture learning involves learning
the *what* and *how* of culture—what to do and how to do it. But
deep-level culture learning involves learning the *why* of culture—
why is American culture the way it is? Why do Americans think
the way they think and behave the way they behave? Deep-level
culture learning is about understanding the worldview assumptions
that result in surface-level cultural structures and behaviors.

Assimilation is the process of entering or becoming part of
the mainstream, dominant culture of the society in which an
immigrant has chosen to live. Some social scientists lump
acculturation and assimilation together as if they were not separate
processes. But they are. It is entirely possible for an immigrant to
achieve a high level of acculturation (culture learning) and yet

resist the process of assimilation, embracing or being absorbed into the mainstream dominant culture.

Being assimilated into another culture requires that the behaviors distinctive of one's home culture fade so deeply into the background (be repressed) that for all practical purposes they cease to function in any meaningful way. Assimilation requires a deep and fundamental change in both surface-level behaviors and deep-level assumptions so that one's original cultural behaviors and assumptions cease to be factors in one's daily life. In other words, assimilation is a process of deep and fundamental change as new perspectives and assumptions are embraced.

Many immigrants resist this kind of deep-level, pervasive change. They learn enough of our culture to be culturally functional, but they resist giving up who they are to become someone else. Their reticence is understandable.

While some immigrants resist the process of assimilation, others embrace it. Some people come to the U.S. with every intention of being assimilated as quickly as possible. They want to become "Americans" in every sense of the word. Most people live between these two extremes, not resisting but not pursuing assimilation, allowing the process to occur naturally, slowly.

Assimilation will usually occur given enough time. Even if a first generation immigrant successfully resists assimilation, his or her children (whether generation 1.5 or generation 2) will likely be assimilated to some degree. By generation 3, a more complete assimilation is nearly inevitable. A family or sub-cultural group has to make a specific and concerted effort to keep their children from being assimilated into mainstream society. Assimilation can be resisted but requires intentional effort.

The issue of assimilation can be confusing. Why would some people want to come to America but not want to become Americans? There are at least two good reasons.

First, just as Americans have a great deal of pride in our cultural heritage, people from other cultures have a great deal of pride in their cultural heritage. When my family and I lived in Nigeria, we did not want to stop being Americans. We were in Nigeria by choice. We loved the people and their culture had much to commend it. The Nigerian people we knew from a number of different tribes were happy, hard working people who loved their families and communities. They tried hard to be good people. We loved our Nigerian friends. But we were Americans and did not want to become Nigerians. Many people who come to America feel pretty much the same way. Most people enjoy a sense of personal identity that is linked, at least in part, to their group identity. Part of my personal identity includes the fact that I am an American. Many people from other cultural contexts link part of their personal identity to their cultural context as well. Even if they choose to live in a different cultural context, their personal identity remains linked to their home culture. They do not want to give up that part of their personal identity any more than most Americans would. This is understandable and should be acceptable.

Second, the older a person is when they begin the acculturation process the harder it is to learn the deep-level part of a new culture. It is difficult to embrace a new value system and new patterns of thinking. It is especially challenging to accept a new set of underlying assumptions. For some people, the new values and new ways of thinking of a second culture just never seem quite right. So they can never be fully embraced.

As Anglo-Americans, we must accept the simple truth that as nice as we are, as rich and powerful as we are, not everybody wants to be us. People want freedom. People want opportunity. But they may not want to stop being who they are to become one of us. And that needs to be acceptable. The assimilationist expectation is, at best, unrealistic for most immigrants.

But surely the assimilation of children who are being educated in American schools is appropriate, especially in the context of multicultural citizenship education. Is it? Should children be expected to abandon their cultural heritage to any degree beyond which they wish to do so? CR as a paradigm for the philosophy of education in multicultural contexts would, with its appropriate focus on cultural sensitivity, allows for stressing acculturation but not demanding assimilation.

A fourth reason CR is an appropriate paradigm for citizenship education in multicultural contexts is because it allows educators to blend an appropriate emphasis on cultural sensitivity with an appropriate focus on the goals of citizenship education. What are the goals of citizenship education? As noted earlier, the goal of citizenship education is to educate students in such a way that they are prepared to make a moral, meaningful contribution to society. Accomplishing this requires appropriate enculturation for American students and meaningful acculturation (but not assimilation) for foreign-born students. What does that mean in a multicultural educational context? Obviously it includes the typical academic skills that are normally associated with a standard education: reading, writing, math, critical thinking skills, history, science, the arts, and social studies.

Social studies (including grade appropriate anthropology) is an especially important part of citizenship education and has been a part of primary and secondary school curriculums for a long time. But in a multicultural context, grade appropriate anthropology needs an even greater emphasis. Why? Because anthropology focuses appropriate attention on and provides students with insights into cultural behaviors that may be different from their own, insights that are essential for meaningful citizenship in any multicultural society. By acknowledging that REALITY is culturally perceived, CR provides a philosophical paradigm for the inclusion of grade appropriate cultural studies in curriculums designed for multicultural contexts.

Summary

CR is a philosophical paradigm that provides a framework for an effective philosophy of education in multicultural contexts. The *realism* aspect of CR acknowledges that there is an objective REALITY independent of human perception that can be studied and understood, one that is subject to empirical and rational analysis and verification. Because rational analysis is part of the construct of CR, questions regarding what is good and right, questions of moral absolutes, will also be part of a CR paradigm. The *critical* aspect of CR acknowledges that perception of that objective REALITY is mind-dependent and therefore culture-dependent as well.

CR is a paradigm that is appropriate for a philosophy of education in multicultural contexts because it is a paradigm that allows for an appropriate scientific methodology in the study of the objective external world, both physical and social, but with an appropriate emphasis on the cultural dynamics involved in inter-ethnic relationships. It is a philosophical paradigm that allows multicultural education to maintain the *citizenship* focus it needs for preparing academically, technologically, and socially capable individuals, individuals who believe in the pursuit of moral, meaningful participation in their community.

CONCLUSION

Over the centuries theories about how to educate children have been developed, defended, discarded, and resurrected or reincarnated. Plato and Aristotle have had lasting influence from the perspective of subject matter, while Rousseau has probably had more influence than many realize regarding methodology, with *Emile* providing the foundation for progressive child-centered approaches. Yet for all the differences in methodology, there is a unity of purpose that pervades educational theory from ancient times to the present. It is the idea (in the broadest terms) that the purpose of education is to prepare an individual for moral and meaningful participation in society. Thus the term *citizenship education.*

For the ancients, a moral person was one focused on inner excellence. A moral person was a happy, thriving person, fulfilling his purpose in life. This was considered a virtuous life.

Education ought to prepare a person for that kind of life, for one of meaningful participation in society, reaching one's full potential as a person, and thereby participating and contributing constructively to the social community of which he or she is a part. How, exactly, this purpose is to be achieved will require protracted and detailed discussions which are beyond the scope of this study. A complicating contemporary issue that must be considered in the discussion is how citizenship education is accomplished in a multicultural, pluralistic social context.

The need for effective multicultural citizenship education exists today and will only become more pressing as we proceed through the early decades of the twenty-first century. Appropriate multicultural curriculum and teaching models are crucial. But even more crucial is teacher training that emphasizes appropriate anthropological training for educators, training that will allow them to develop an understanding of the importance of the worldview assumptions of the various ethnic groups present in their classrooms.

This study of a philosophy of education in multicultural contexts has focused attention on three considerations: 1) the philosophy of education that drives the purposes and goals of the enterprise, 2) the factors that are related to the multicultural realities of our contemporary society as it relates to teacher training, and 3) the need for a philosophical paradigm that provides an appropriate framework from which educators can work toward the goal of effective citizenship education. We have discussed the philosophy of education aspect: the goal of education is to produce morally sound citizens who can participate in meaningful, productive ways in society. We have also addressed the multicultural concerns. To accomplish effective multicultural citizenship education teachers in multicultural contexts must be anthropologically informed, understanding the worldviews and cultures of the students in their classrooms. And we have discussed the third concern, an appropriate paradigm from which effective citizenship education may be accomplished. CR is an appropriate paradigm for multicultural citizenship education for two basic reasons.

First the *realism* aspect of CR focuses attention on the objective nature of RELAITY, a REALITY that it can be studied and understood. Objective insights can be ascertained, even though the ascertaining involves subjective perception. The subjective perception of objective REALITY does not diminish the objective nature of the REALITY being perceived. This perspective is essential for ongoing scientific research (in an increasingly technological context) and for preparing individuals for meaningful and just participation in a diverse global community.

Second, the *critical* aspect of CR recognizes the role of culture in the way we perceive and respond to REALITY. Because perception of the real world (objective REALITY) is mind-dependent it is also culture-dependent, for culture (specifically the underlying assumptions on which culture is built—worldview) shapes the mind. In recognizing this, CR encourages educators to develop and nurture in themselves and their students a deep appreciation of the role of culture in our lives. Because CR recognizes the role of culture in the perception and interpretation of REALITY, it acknowledges the subjective aspect of life and thus encourages the development of toleration for and sensitivity to different cultural perspectives. Yet the focus on ascertaining objective REALITY provides a platform not only for empirical research of the material world, but also for the rational pursuit of the good life, that is, what it means to be a moral person contributing to the good of the society in which one lives.

The dual focus of CR makes it an appropriate paradigm for accomplishing citizenship education in multicultural contexts.

Citizenship education in multicultural contexts is a multifaceted complex enterprise. To accomplish it requires: 1) a clear vision of the process and the purposes, 2) professional educators thoroughly trained not only in the subject matter they will teach but also in cultural anthropology and cross-cultural fieldwork so they can understand the culturally-other dynamic present in their classrooms, and 3) a philosophical paradigm that is specific enough to provide a framework for accomplishing the task but flexible enough (or broad enough) to allow for creativity and dynamic development in a context that continues to evolve. CR provides the flexible framework educators need to accomplish multicultural citizenship education in a scientifically advanced, pluralistic society.

WORKS CITED

Angeles, Peter A. *The Harper Collins Dictionary of Philosophy*. 2nd ed. New York: Harper Collins, 1992).

Aristotle. "Nicomachean Ethics." trans. W. D. Ross. *The Basic Works of Aristotle*. Ed. Richard McKeon. New York: The Modern Library, 2001.

Banks, James A. *Educating Citizens in a Multicultural Society*. New York: Teachers College Press, 1997.

---   *An Introduction to Multicultural Education*. Boston: Pearson, 2008.
Barrow, Robin and Ronald Woods. *An Introduction to Philosophy of Education*. 4th ed. London: Routledge, 2006.

Bhaskar, Roy. "General Introduction." *Critical Realism: Essential Readings*. Ed. Margaret Archer. London: Routledge, 1998.

Blackburn, Simon. "Idealism." *Oxford Dictionary of Philosophy*. Oxford: Oxford University Press, 1996.

Buchler, Justice. *Philosophical Writings of Peirce*. New York: Dover Publications, 1955.

Carrithers, Michael. "Culture." *The Dictionary of Anthropology*. Ed. Thomas Barfield. Malden: Blackwell, 1997.

Cooper, David E. "Plato." *Fifty Major Thinkers on Education: From Confucius to Dewey*. Ed. Joy A. Palmer. London: Routledge, 2001.

Cooper, John, M. "Protagoras." *Plato: The Complete Works*. Ed. John M. Cooper. Indianapolis: Hackett Publishing Company, 1997.

Crane, Tim. "Idealism." *Western Philosophy: An Illustrated Guide*. Ed. David Papineau. Oxford: Oxford University Press, 2004.

---   "Berkeley." *Western Philosophy: An Illustrated Guide*. Ed. David Papineau. Oxford: Oxford University Press, 2004.

Cruickshank, Justin. *Critical Realism: The Difference it Makes*. Ed. Justin Cruickshank. London: Routledge, 2003.

Cushner, Kenneth, Averil McClelland, and Philip Stafford. *Human Diversity in Education: An Integrative Approach*. 3rd ed. Boston: McGraw/Hill, 2000.

Delaney, C.F. "Critical Realism." *The Cambridge Dictionary of Philosophy*. Ed. Robert Audi. Cambridge: Cambridge University Press, 1999.

Dewey, John. "What The School Is." *Philosophical Documents in Education*. Ronald Reed and Tony Johnson. New York: Longman, 2000.

Dhillon, Pradeep and J. Mark Halstead. "Multicultural Education." *The Blackwell Guide to the Philosophy of Education*. Malden: Blackwell, 2003.

Duarte, Valerie and Thomas Reed. "Learning to Teach in Urban Settings." *Annual Editions: Multicultural Education 06/07*. Dubuque: McGraw-Hill, 2006.

Fitzpatrick, P. J. "Saint Augustine." *Fifty Major Thinkers on Education: From Confucius to Dewey*. Ed. Joy A. Palmer. London: Routledge, 2001.

Green, Stanton W. and Stephen M Perlman. "Education, Diversity, and American Culture." *Cultural Diversity in the United States*. Ed. Larry Naylor. Westport: Bergin and Garvey, 1997.

Gruber, Frederick. *Historical and Contemporary Philosophies of Education*. New York:Thomas Y. Cromwell Company, 1973.

Harris, R. Baine. "Neoplatonism." *The Oxford Companion to Philosophy*. 2nd ed. Oxford: Oxford University Press, 2005.

Heil, John. "Direct Realism." *The Cambridge Dictionary of Philosophy*. Ed. Robert Audi. Cambridge: Cambridge University Press, 1999.

Hepburn, R.W. "Relativism, Ethical." *The Oxford Companion to Philosophy*. 2nd ed. Ed. Ted Honderich. Oxford: Oxford University Press, 2005.

Hiebert, Paul G. *Cultural Anthropology*. Grand Rapids: Baker, 1983.

--- "The Gospel in Our Culture: Methods of Social and Cultural Analysis." *The Church Between Gospel and Culture: The Emerging Mission in North America.* Eds. George Hunsberger and Craig Van Gelder. Grand Rapids: Eerdmans, 1996.

--- *Missiological Implications of Epistemological Shifts: Affirming Truth in a Modern/Postmodern World.* Harrisburg: Trinity International Press, 1999.

Hirst, R. J. "Realism." *The Encyclopedia of Philosophy.* Ed. Paul Edwards. New York: McMillan, 1967.

Hobson, Peter. "Aristotle." *Fifty Major Thinkers on Education: From Confucius to Dewey.* Ed. Joy A. Palmer. London: Routledge, 2001.

Holmes, Arthur F. *Ethics: Approaching Moral Decisions.* 2nd ed. Downers Grove: InterVarsity Press, 2007.

Jenks, Charles, James O. Lee, and Barry Kanpol. "Approaches to Multicultural Education in Preservice Teacher Education: Philosophical Frameworks and Models for Teaching." *Multicultural Education: Annual Editions, 02-03.* Ed Fred Schultz. Guilford: McGraw/Hill/Dushkin, 2002.

Jupp, James. "Culturally Relevant Teaching: One Teacher's Journey Through Theory And Practice." *Annual Editions: Multicultural Education 06/07.* Dubuque: McGraw-Hill, 2006.

Karney, Michael. *World View.* Novato: Chandler and Sharp, 1984.

Knight, George. *Philosophy and Education: An Introduction in Christian Perspective.* Berrien Springs: Andrews University Press, 2006.

Kraft, Charles H. *Anthropology for Christian Witness.* Maryknoll: Orbis, 1996.

--- *Worldview for Christian Witness.* Prepublication Edition, 2002.

Kuhn, Thomas S. *The Structure of Scientific Revolutions.* 3rd ed. Chicago: University of Chicago Press, 1996.

Lopez, Jose and Garry Potter. *After Postmodernism: An Introduction to Critical Realism.* London: Continuum, 2001.

116

Noddings, Nel. *Philosophy of Education*. Boulder: Westview Press, 2007.

---   "The Challenge to Care in Schools: An Alternative Approach to Education." *Philosophical Documents in Education.* Ronal Reed and Tony Johnson. New York: Longman, 2000.

O'Hagan, Timothy. "Jean-Jacques Rousseau." *Fifty Major Thinkers on Education: From Confucius to Dewey.* Ed. Joy A. Palmer. London: Routledge, 2001.

Plato. *Laws*, Bk. II, Sec. 659D. *Plato: The Complete Works.* Ed. John M. Cooper. trans. Trevor J. Sanders. Indianapolis: Hackett Publishing Company, 1997.

Reed, Ronald F. and Tony W. Johnson. *Philosophical Documents in Education.* New York: Longman, 2000.

Rescher, Nicholas. "Idealism." *The Cambridge Dictionary of Philosophy.* Ed. Robert Audi. Cambridge: Cambridge University Press, 1999.

Rogers, Glenn. *The Role of Worldview in Mission and Multiethnic Ministry.* Bedford: Mission and Ministry Resources, 2002.

---   *Understanding American Culture: The Theological and Philosophical Shaping of the American Worldview*, Mission and Ministry Resources, 2006.

---   *Evangelizing Immigrants: Outreach and Ministry Among Immigrants and their Children.* Bedford: Mission and Ministry Resources, 2006.

Williams, Norma. "Multiculturalism: Issues for the Twenty-First Century." *Cultural Diversity in the United States.* Ed. Larry Naylor. Westport: Bergin and Garvey, 1997.

Printed in the United Kingdom by
Lightning Source UK Ltd., Milton Keynes
138833UK00002B/208/P